T0306624

WORKBOOK

Eoin Higgins and Philip Wood

CAMBRIDGE
UNIVERSITY PRESS

University Printing House, Cambridge CB2 8BS, United Kingdom

One Liberty Plaza, 20th Floor, New York, NY 10006, USA

477 Williamstown Road, Port Melbourne, VIC 3207, Australia

314–321, 3rd Floor, Plot 3, Splendor Forum, Jasola District Centre, New Delhi – 110025, India

79 Anson Road, #06–04/06, Singapore 079906

José Abascal, 56 – 1°, 28003 Madrid, Spain

Avenida Paulista, 807 conjunto 2315, 01311 -915, São Paulo, Brazi

Torre de los Parques, Colonia Tlacoquemécatl del Valle, Mexico City, CP 03200, Mexico

Cambridge University Press is part of the University of Cambridge.

It furthers the University's mission by disseminating knowledge in the pursuit of education, learning and research at the highest international levels of excellence.

www.cambridge.org
Information on this title: www.cambridge.org/9781108810593

First published 2020

20 19 18 17 16 15 14 13 12 11 10 9 8 7 6 5 4 3 2 1

Printed in Great Britain by CPI Group (UK) Ltd, Croydon CR0 4YY

A catalogue record for this publication is available from the British Library
ISBN 978-1-108-81059-3 Shape it! Workbook Level 4
ISBN 978-1-108-72655-9 Own it! Workbook Level 4

Additional resources for this publication at www.cambridge.org/shapeit

Cambridge University Press has no responsibility for the persistence or accuracy of URLs for external or third-party internet websites referred to in this publication, and does not guarantee that any content on such websites is, or will remain, accurate or appropriate. Information regarding prices, travel timetables, and other factual information given in this work is correct at the time of first printing but Cambridge University Press does not guarantee the accuracy of such information thereafter.

CONTENTS

WELCOME!

VOCABULARY AND READING
Travel

1 ⭐ **Match the words with the definitions.**

> accommodation   backpacking
> resort   sightseeing
> tourist attractions   ~~trip~~

1 a journey where you visit a place for a short time and then come back again ____trip____

2 visiting places that are interesting because they are historical, famous, etc.
_____

3 traveling or walking, carrying your things in a bag on your back _____

4 monuments or places that people on vacation like to visit _____

5 a town or place where people go on vacation, very often next to the ocean _____

6 a place where you live or stay
_____

2 ⭐ **Complete the sentences with information that is true for you. (See the *Learn to Learn* tip in the Student's Book, p4.)**

1 _____ is a famous tourist attraction in my country.

2 For our accommodation on our last vacation, we stayed in _____ .

3 _____ is a popular resort in my country.

4 The last trip I went on was to _____ .

5 In my opinion, going backpacking is a _____ way to spend your vacation.

6 I would like to go sightseeing in _____ .

Music and Theater

3 ⭐⭐ **Complete the text. The first letter of each word is given.**

I was very surprised when Ms. Bayliss gave me the biggest
¹part_____ in the school musical. It wasn't easy to learn
all my ²l_____ , but after several ³r_____ ,
I knew them perfectly. I was nervous on the day of the
⁴s_____ because my whole family was in the
⁵a_____ . But everything went well, and after the final
⁶s_____ , everyone stood up and clapped!

An Interview

4 ⭐ **Read the interview. What did Jed do on vacation? Choose the correct photo.**

 a ☐

 b ☐

MIA So, where did you go on vacation, Jed?

JED Italy – it was a fantastic trip!

MIA Did you stay at a resort?

JED No, it was a hotel. We did a lot of sightseeing. We went to some famous tourist attractions, like the Colosseum in Rome. It was amazing!

MIA So, what was the best part of your trip?

JED Oh, that was when we saw an opera: *The Barber of Seville* in the Teatro Argentina – it's almost 300 years old! It's an amazing place – so beautiful!

MIA But wasn't the opera in Italian?

JED Yes, it was, and most of the audience was Italian, but there were subtitles.

5 ⭐⭐ **Read the interview again and answer the questions.**

1 Where did Jed stay?
_____

2 What did Jed think of the Colosseum?
_____

3 What else did Jed do in Rome?
_____

4 Why could Jed understand the opera?
_____

GRAMMAR IN ACTION AND VOCABULARY

Past and Present, Simple and Continuous

1 ⭐⭐ **Write the sentences in the past.**

1 Dan is reading the paper.

Dan was reading the paper.

2 They aren't listening to music.

_____

3 Am I making a lot of noise?

_____

4 Beth usually plays soccer on Saturdays.

_____

5 They don't live in an apartment.

_____

6 Does Michael like school?

_____

2 ⭐⭐ **Complete the conversation with the verbs in the box in the correct tense.**

~~be~~ do enjoy have help visit

A How ¹ ___was___ your trip to Paris?

B Great, thanks! I ² _____ it a lot!

A What ³ _____ you _____ there?

B We ⁴ _____ a lot of tourist attractions!

A You're so lucky! While you ⁵ _____ a great time in Paris, I ⁶ _____ my dad paint the house!

3 ⭐⭐⭐ **Answer the questions with information that is true for you.**

1 What did you do last weekend?

_____

2 What were you doing at nine o'clock last night?

_____

3 What does your dad do?

_____

4 What's your mom probably doing at the moment?

_____

Ways of Communicating

4 ⭐ **Circle eight more communication verbs in the word snake.**

postshoutwhisperdescribesmiletranslateshakehandsgreetwave

5 ⭐⭐ **Complete the chart with the verbs from Exercise 4. Some verbs go in both columns.**

You Can Use Your Hands to Do This	You Can Use Your Mouth to Do This
1 _____post_____	6 _____
2 _____	7 _____
3 _____	8 _____
4 _____	9 _____
5 _____	10 _____
	11 _____

6 ⭐⭐ **Complete the sentences with the verbs from Exercise 4.**

1 Do you know anyone who can ___translate___ from English into Chinese?

2 Did you _____ a comment on my blog?

3 Please don't _____ ! I can hear you!

4 How would you _____ your personality?

5 When you _____ , you feel happier.

6 If you don't know the answer when the teacher asks you, I'll _____ it to you very quietly.

7 When movie stars arrive at the Oscars, they often _____ to the crowd.

8 When I have my interview tomorrow, how should I _____ the person who is interviewing me? Should I _____ with them?

LISTENING AND GRAMMAR IN ACTION

A Conversation

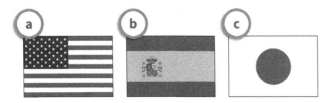

1 ⭐⭐ Match the flags a–c with the countries 1–3.

1 Spain ___   2 Japan ___   3 the U.S.A. ___

🎧 **2** S.01 ⭐ Listen to the conversation. Which of the countries from Exercise 1 does the girl's dad sometimes go to?

_____

🎧 **3** S.01 ⭐⭐ Listen again. Put the pictures a–f in the order that they are mentioned.

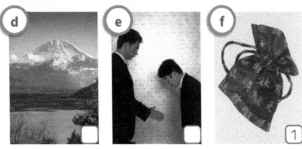

4 ⭐⭐⭐ Answer the questions.

1 Which country would you like to visit? Why?

_____

2 Would you like to travel a lot for your job? Why?

_____

3 Do you think people smile a lot in your country? Give a reason for your answer.

_____

Present Perfect and Simple Past

5 ⭐ Complete the sentences with the words in the box. There are two extra words.

at   ever   for   from   ~~have~~   never   's   since

1 ___Have___ you finished the book?
2 We've been here _____ four o'clock.
3 Have you _____ been to Japan?
4 John's studied French _____ three years.
5 I've _____ seen snow before.
6 Beth _____ sent me a message.

6 ⭐⭐ Circle the correct options.

1 Last year, I *went* / *'ve been* to London.
2 *Did you ever climb* / *Have you ever climbed* a mountain?
3 My sister *liked* / *'s liked* chocolate since she was a baby.
4 I *didn't do* / *haven't done* my homework. I'm going to start now!
5 I *called* / *'ve called* you just a minute ago!
6 We *were* / *'ve been* at the mall for three hours now!

7 ⭐⭐ Complete the text with the simple past or present perfect form of the verb in parentheses.

● ● ●

TO: Aidan

FROM: Paola

Hi Aidan,
I ¹ _'ve been_ (be) in Rome for almost a week now.
I ² _____ (arrive) last Friday. My Italian
³ _____ (not get) much better, which
isn't very surprising, really. I need more time.
I ⁴ _____ (do) a lot of sightseeing!
Yesterday I ⁵ _____ (go) to the Vatican
The museum is incredible! I ⁶ _____
(eat) some very good food because the woman
I'm staying with is a great cook. Last night she
⁷ _____ (make) *cannelloni al ragù.*
Tomorrow, I start at the language school. I
⁸ _____ (not feel) so happy or excited
for a long time!
Love, Paola

WRITING
An Informal Email

1 ⭐ **Read Jack's email to his friend Ethan. Which two of the activities in the pictures a–c did he do?**

TO: Ethan@postit.com

FROM: Jack@comunica.com

SUBJECT: News!

¹Hi Ethan,

1 ²How are things? Are you enjoying life in Mexico? ³I just wanted to get in contact because I haven't sent you an email for a long time. Sorry about that!

2 I've been really busy lately. I'm in the school play, and we've had a lot of rehearsals after school. I have a big part, so it hasn't been easy to learn all my lines! But I think I've finally managed to do it. I hope so because the play's next week! Have you ever done any acting? Perhaps you can give me some advice!

3 Last Saturday was my dad's 50th birthday, so he took us all out for a meal in a really nice restaurant in the country. All his brothers and sisters came, and everyone gave him a present. I gave him a D.C. United soccer scarf because he's a big fan. I think he liked it!

4 So, that's my news. When are you coming back to visit?

⁴Bye for now!

⁵Take care,

Jack

---

2 ⭐⭐ **Read the email again. Match the paragraphs (1–4) with the information (A–D).**

A   say goodbye ☐

B   things Jack has done recently ☐

C   things Jack did at a particular time ☐

D   say hello and why you're writing ☐

3 ⭐⭐ **Look at paragraphs 2 and 3 again. What tenses does Jack use to describe his actions? Why?**

_____

_____

_____

4 ⭐⭐ **Match the underlined phrases in the email 1–5 with the phrases a–e.**

a Love, ☐   d See you soon! ☐

b I'm writing to ☐ e How are you? ☐

c Hello ☐

PLAN

5 ⭐⭐ **Write an email to a friend in the U.S.A., telling them what you've done recently. Make two lists.**

   1 Things I've done when the exact time is not important or that are not finished (present perfect):

   _____

   _____

   _____

   2 Things I did at a particular time (simple past):

   _____

   _____

   _____

WRITE

6 ⭐⭐⭐ **Write your email. Remember to include four paragraphs, your ideas from Exercise 5, vocabulary from this unit, and phrases from the *Useful Language* box (see Student's Book, p9).**

CHECK

7 **Do you ...**
- start and end the email correctly?
- give the reason why you are writing?
- use verbs in the correct tense?

1 What is fashion?

VOCABULARY
Describing Clothes and Shoes

1 ⭐ (Circle) the correct adjectives to describe the clothes.

1
a *cotton* / (*denim*) skirt

2
a *tight* / *baggy* sweater

3
a *plain* / *checkered* shirt

4
baggy / *high-heeled* boots

5
a *striped* / *flowery* T-shirt

6
a *long-sleeved* / *polka-dot* dress

2 ⭐⭐ Complete the conversations with the words in the box. There are two extra words.

> cotton   checkered   denim   flowery
> high-heeled   leather   long-sleeved   ~~tight~~

1 **A** Are those shorts OK?
  B No, I need a bigger size. They're very _____tight_____!

2 **A** Do you want a plain or a checkered T-shirt?
  B No, I want something really different! That _____ one is nice!

3 **A** What do you usually wear in the summer?
  B Cool clothes made of _____!

4 **A** Do you like my new black and white _____ shirt?
  B Not really! It looks like a chess board!

5 **A** Are you going to pack some jeans for your trip to Córdoba?
  B Are you joking? It's 40°C there at the moment! I don't want to wear anything made of _____!

6 **A** How often do you wear _____ shoes?
  B Not often. Only when I go to a party or formal dinner.

3 ⭐ Match the adjectives 1–5 with the categories a–c. (See the *Learn to Learn* tip in the Student's Book, p11.)

1 baggy, tight
2 checkered, striped   a material
3 denim, cotton   b pattern
4 high-heeled, long-sleeved   c shape
5 plain, polka-dot

4 ⭐⭐ Put the words in the correct order.

1 a / checkered / red and green / shirt
  a red and green checkered shirt

2 a / skirt / denim / plain
  _____

3 jeans / cotton / tight / white
  _____

4 jacket / denim / red / baggy / a
  _____

5 striped / brown and blue / T-shirt / a / tight / cotton
  _____
  _____

6 brown and white / shoes / leather / polka-dot / high-heeled
  _____
  _____

5 ⭐⭐⭐ Write four sentences about clothes that you like and don't like to wear. Use adjectives from Exercise 1.

_____
_____
_____
_____

Explore It! 🖱

Guess the correct answer.

In what decade did miniskirts become popular?

a the 1950s   b the 1960s   c the 1970s

Find another interesting fact about popular fashion in a past decade. Write a question and send it to a classmate in an email, or ask them in the next class.

READING
A Blog Entry

1 ⭐ Look at the text quickly and (circle) the correct answers.

1 The text is *a an advertisement* / *a personal opinion*.

2 It's about *how often to wash jeans* / *what jeans to buy*.

2 ⭐⭐ Read the blog entry. Check the meaning of the words in the box in a dictionary. Then complete the sentences.

> brand   claim   ~~eliminate~~   harm   research   turn out

1 Cheese gives me a headache. I need to __eliminate__ it from my diet.

2 Don't wash that shirt in very hot water. It will definitely _____ the material!

3 I'm going to do some _____ before I buy a new phone.

4 I like these jeans, but I don't know this _____. Is it any good?

5 Some people _____ that shopping online is 100 percent safe, but I'm not so sure.

6 I'm making a dress, but I have a feeling that it's not going to _____ well.

3 ⭐⭐ Are the sentences *T* (true) or *F* (false)? Correct the false sentences.

1 In the writer's opinion, the question of how often to wash jeans is very important.

   F It's not the most important topic in the world.

2 The writer agrees with her friend about how often to wash jeans.

   _____

3 In the writer's opinion, an important person in the clothing industry has a strange idea.

   _____

4 Freezing jeans is a good way to clean them.

   _____

5 It's best not to wash your jeans too often.

   _____

6 The experts make a good recommendation.

   _____

4 ⭐⭐⭐ Do you think the information in the blog entry is useful and interesting? Why / Why not?

_____

_____

_____

● ● ●

NEW YORK CALLING!   BLOG | ABOUT ME | CONTACT ME

TO WASH OR NOT TO WASH JEANS?
THAT IS THE QUESTION!

I haven't written an entry recently because I've been taking exams all week! Did you miss me? Today, I want to talk about a very important subject: how often to wash denim jeans! OK, maybe it's not the most important topic in the world, but people have very different ideas about it. One of my friends even thinks that you should never wash jeans because it harms them. I don't know about that! Imagine wearing a pair of tight jeans that you haven't washed for over a year! So, anyway, I decided to do some research online about how often you should actually wash jeans. One thing I read really surprised me: the head of a company that makes a very well-known brand of jeans says that he hardly ever washes his. He just puts them in the freezer. He claims that this keeps them clean! Speaking personally, I wouldn't want to put my jeans next to a bag of frozen peas! And it turns out that the "freezer theory" isn't correct. After you wear your jeans just once, they're covered in bacteria, skin cells, and the natural oils from your body. And freezing them won't eliminate these things. According to the experts, there is one good reason for not washing your jeans very often: they get a little baggier every time you wash them. And most of us don't want to wear baggy jeans! Experts actually say there's no specific recommended frequency for washing jeans – but you should definitely wash them when they start to smell! That sounds like good advice to me!

GRAMMAR IN ACTION
Present Perfect Simple and Present Perfect Continuous

1 ⭐⭐ **Match the beginnings of the sentences 1–6 with the ends a–f.**

1 I've done — `b`
2 Jack's been playing soccer ☐
3 Have they had ☐
4 You've been wearing ☐
5 Bethany hasn't been going ☐
6 Has your dad finished cleaning ☐

a that shirt all week!
b all my homework.
c the bathroom?
d for three hours!
e lunch yet?
f to the gym recently.

2 ⭐⭐ **Complete the sentences with the verbs in parentheses. Use the present perfect simple (PPS) or present perfect continuous (PPC).**

1 We _haven't made_ (not make) lunch yet. (PPS)
2 I _____ (do) a lot of clothes shopping recently. (PPC)
3 Ana _____ (visit) her family. (PPC)
4 _____ (they / finish) the game? (PPS)
5 My tablet _____ (not work) all day. (PPC)
6 My aunt _____ (have) a lot of different jobs. (PPS)

3 ⭐⭐ (Circle) **the correct options.**

1 I've *felt* / (*been feeling*) very tired recently.
2 John hasn't *answered* / *been answering* my last email.
3 Rachel isn't here. Has she *gone* / *been going* shopping?
4 Our neighbors have *made* / *been making* a lot of noise.
5 Why have *you bought* / *you been buying* three baggy sweaters?
6 *Did you study* / *Have you been studying* for your exams all week?

4 ⭐⭐ **Write sentences in the present perfect simple or continuous.**

1 what / you / do / recently?
What have you been doing recently?
2 I / finish / finally / my school project!
_____
3 Nick / wear / the same clothes / all week.
_____
4 you / ever / be / to Los Angeles?
_____
5 I / try / to contact you / all day!
_____
6 Jan / not decide / what to do
_____

5 ⭐⭐⭐ **Complete the messages with the correct form of the verbs in the box.**

| find   go shopping   ~~look for~~   not buy   try on   wait |

You ¹ _'ve been looking for_ a dress for the party for a long time! ² _____ you _____ anything yet?   Maxine

No! And I ³ _____ for hours!
I ⁴ _____ six different dresses, but I ⁵ _____ anything yet!   Sarah

Well, I ⁶ _____ for you in the café for too long! I'm leaving!
                    Maxine

6 ⭐⭐⭐ **Write a sentence about something that you have or haven't done before and a sentence about something that you have or haven't been doing recently.**

I've never been to Seattle.
I've been playing a lot of video games recently.
_____
_____
_____

VOCABULARY AND LISTENING
Verbs Related to Clothes and Shoes

1 ⭐ **Circle the correct options.**

1 These pants are very tight. They don't (fit) / look good on me.

2 Can you please *hang* / *fit* up the pants over there?

3 Could you help me *unzip* / *fold* my dress. I want to take it off.

4 People will still wear jeans in 100 years. They will never *wear out* / *go out of style*.

5 Do these shoes *go with* / *wear out* this dress?

6 You look great with those earrings. They really *match* / *look good on* you!

2 ⭐⭐ **Complete the text with words and phrases from Exercise 1.**

HOW TO LOOK GOOD!

● Some clothes [1] _go out of style_ quickly! So, don't wear something that was popular last year!

● Your clothes must [2] _____ you perfectly! Don't buy something that you really like if it isn't the right size!

● Buy clothes with "easy" colors that [3] _____ a lot of other colors.

● Know what kinds of clothes [4] _____ you! Some people look great in stripes – but do you?

● Don't [5] _____ your clothes and put them in drawers. It's much better if you [6] _____ them _____ .

3 ⭐⭐⭐ **Write sentences that are true for you. (See the *Learn to Learn* tip in the Student's Book, p14.)**

1 How quickly do you wear out your clothes?

_____

2 Do all your clothes fit you well? Give details.

_____

3 What colors look good on you? Why?

_____

4 Do you ever wear clothes that have gone out of style? Why / Why not?

_____

An Interview

🎧 1.01 **4** ⭐ **Listen to Caitlin talking about her job as a salesperson. Put the things she talks about in the correct order.**

a ☐ the bad points of the job

b ☐ the good points of the job

c ☐ why she wanted to work as a salesperson

🎧 1.01 **5** ⭐⭐ **Listen again and circle the correct options.**

1 Why did Caitlin decide to work as a salesperson in a clothing store?

  a She wants to work as a fashion designer.

  (b) She's very interested in clothes.

  c She likes helping people.

2 What are Caitlin's coworkers like?

  a They're nice.

  b Some are nice; some aren't.

  c She really likes her boss.

3 What happens every one or two months?

  a She buys clothes at a discount.

  b She helps with window displays.

  c New clothes arrive at the store.

4 How much of a discount does Caitlin get?

  a 15 percent

  b 50 percent

  c It depends on the clothes.

5 What are two negative aspects of the job?

  a Some of the jobs are a bit boring, and the pay isn't very good.

  b Some of the customers can be rude, and you're standing up all the time.

  c Some customers aren't polite, and not all the jobs are interesting.

GRAMMAR IN ACTION
Modifiers

1 ⭐ **Read the phrases and circle the options that have the same meaning.**

1 absolutely wrong
   (a) totally wrong   b a bit wrong
2 fairly nice
   a extremely nice   b pretty nice
3 a lot more difficult
   a a bit more difficult   b far more difficult
4 a bit bigger
   a a little bigger   b far bigger
5 extremely tired
   a pretty tired   b really tired
6 pretty far
   a fairly far   b extremely far

2 ⭐⭐ **Look at the information from a price comparison website. Are the sentences *T* (true) or *F* (false)?**

1 Exclu jeans are extremely expensive. T
2 Exclu jeans are far more expensive than Basic Co jeans. ___
3 Basic Co jeans aren't really cheap. ___
4 Wright Brothers jeans are a bit less expensive than Exclu jeans. ___
5 Basic Co jeans are pretty expensive. ___

3 ⭐⭐ **Circle the correct options.**

1 These pants aren't "a little" baggy. They're *pretty* / *extremely* baggy!
2 Your watch was a bit more expensive than mine, but it's *a little* / *far* better! It's fantastic!
3 I'm *pretty* / *really* hungry, but I'm not very hungry.
4 The weather was *a bit* / *far* hotter than we imagined. It was a big surprise.
5 Mike's *fairly* / *really* generous. I think he's the most generous person I know.
6 I'm *fairly* / *totally* sure that the store's closed today, but maybe I'm wrong.

4 ⭐⭐ **Complete the conversation with the missing words. Circle the correct options.**

A How was your vacation in San Sebastian?
B Only ¹_____ good, I'm afraid.
A So, not ²_____ fantastic?
B No. The weather was ³_____ terrible. It rained all the time!
A Oh, no! What about the food? I've heard it's fantastic there – ⁴_____ better than the food in the U.S.A.!
B Yes, it was ⁵_____ delicious! I think it was ⁶_____ more expensive than the U.S.A., but my dad said the prices weren't too bad.

1 a totally   (b) fairly   c far
2 a a lot   b fairly   c absolutely
3 a really   b a bit   c a little
4 a pretty   b far   c a little
5 a absolutely   b pretty   c a lot
6 a far   b really   c a bit

5 ⭐⭐⭐ **Complete the sentences so they are true for you. Use modifiers from this page.**

1 Living in my hometown is _____
2 My family is _____
3 For me, buying clothes is _____.
4 When I compare English and math, I think English is _____
5 In my opinion, soccer is _____.
6 When I compare drinking water or soda, I think _____

WRITING
A Blog Comment

● ● ●

FIVE WAYS TO SPEND LESS MONEY ON CLOTHES

- Go to secondhand stores!
- Buy your clothes online!
- Swap clothes with friends!
- Only buy clothes on sale!
- Buy clothes with neutral colors (black, gray, or white). They'll go well with all your other clothes!

Great post! Thanks for sharing! TBH, I've always thought that buying clothes online was a bit dangerous. I mean, what happens if you get something and it doesn't fit you? That's a problem! But since reading your post, I've looked at some online clothing sites, and they really help you find the right size. What's more, some of the clothes are extremely inexpensive, especially if you buy from China or Hong Kong! I've just bought a flowery dress online, and it fits me perfectly! It's absolutely amazing!   Sonya

Your post really got me thinking about how to save money on clothes! I've been spending too much recently, so it's become a BIG problem! IMO, going to secondhand stores is a really good idea. I had no idea that they had such great stuff! I thought they only had clothes that were out of style! I've already bought a great denim shirt and a cool polka-dot T-shirt. And I've decided to get all my clothes from secondhand stores in the future! They're far cheaper!   Aidan

1 ⭐⭐ **Read the blog entry and the comments and answer the questions.**

1 What is the blog entry about?

_____

2 Which ideas from the blog have Sonya and Aidan used?

_____

2 ⭐⭐ **Read the comments again and answer the questions in your notebook.**

1 What do *TBH* and *IMO* mean?

2 Why does Sonya use an exclamation point in: *It's absolutely amazing!* ?

3 Why does Aidan use capital letters in: *It's become a BIG problem!* ?

3 ⭐⭐ **Complete the *Useful Language* phrases. Look at the <u>underlined</u> phrases in the blog for help.**

1 You really __got__ me thinking about how much I spend.

2 I've been thinking and I've _____ to go shopping far less often.

3 Great _____! Thanks for _____!

4 I had _____ that buying online was so easy!

5 _____ reading your post, I've really started to think about how I shop.

PLAN

4 ⭐⭐ **Write your own blog comment. Choose one of the five ideas from the blog entry and take notes about these things.**

Do you like the idea? Why / Why not? _____

_____

Other ideas you would like to try in the future:

_____

WRITE

5 ⭐⭐⭐ **Write your comment. Remember to include the present perfect simple and continuous, modifiers, vocabulary from this unit, phrases from the *Useful Language* box (see Student's Book, p.17), and the features from Exercise 2.**

CHECK

6 **Do you ...**

- explain why an idea might or might not work well?
- explain what you would like to try in the future?

VOCABULARY

1 Complete the crossword. Use the clues.

DOWN ↓

1 _____-_____ shoes
4 _____-_____ top
5 _____ skirt
6 _____ T-shirt
8 _____ shoes

ACROSS →

2 _____ pants
3 _____ shirt
6 _____ scarf
7 _____-_____ dress
9 _____ sweater
10 _____ jeans
11 _____ skirt

2 Complete the sentences with the words in the box.

> fit   fold   go out of style   go with   hang up
> look good on   match   unzip   wear out   zip up

1 I don't think these shoes will _____
  soon. Sneakers are always popular.

2 You need to _____ your coat. It's
  very cold!

3 These shorts don't _____ me now,
  but they weren't too small last year!

4 Do you think these earrings _____
  the color of my eyes?

5 I never wear brown. It doesn't
  _____ me.

6 I only _____ shirts when I pack
  a bag. I always _____ them
  _____ at home.

7 That shirt doesn't _____ those
  pants. They look terrible together!

8 You can _____ the zipper on the
  tent. It isn't raining anymore.

9 Those are nice shoes, so please don't play
  soccer in them. You'll _____ them
  _____ very quickly!

GRAMMAR IN ACTION

3 Complete the sentences with the present perfect simple or continuous form of the verbs in parentheses.

1 I _____ (not see) that movie. Is it good?

2 Claudia _____ (try) to buy tickets all afternoon!

3 Oh, no! I _____ (lose) my earring!

4 Dan _____ (never / play) chess.

5 I _____ (finish)! I'm sorry you _____ (wait) so long.

6 _____ (we / buy) everything we need?

4 Read the conversations and ⟨circle⟩ the correct options.

1 A How was the party?
  B It was *really / pretty* good, but not amazing.

2 A Did you enjoy the movie!
  B Yes, it was *fairly / absolutely* amazing!

3 A How are you feeling?
  B Only *a little / a lot* better.

4 A Did you do well on your exams?
  B My results were *extremely / pretty* good, but they weren't fantastic.

5 A This school project is hard!
  B Yes, it is! It's *fairly / far* harder than Ms. Taylor said!

6 A I'm the best player on the team!
  B I'm sorry, but you're *fairly / totally* wrong about that!

CUMULATIVE LANGUAGE

5 Complete the email with the missing words. ⟨Circle⟩ the correct options.

TO: Amy	FROM: Zoe

Hi Amy,

How are you? I'm sorry that I ¹_____ for a while. I have a lot of news! I ²_____ a course in fashion design, and it ³_____ really well! I ⁴_____ on a dress with a flowery design all week. I ⁵_____ it because it's ⁶_____ hard work. But I love it!

I ⁷_____ that I want to work as a fashion designer in the future. I think it would be a ⁸_____ awesome job – and ⁹_____ more interesting than working in an office! How about you? ¹⁰_____ life in Chile? Your Spanish must be ¹¹_____ fantastic now because it was ¹²_____ good before!

Anyway, talk to you soon!

Zoe

1 a haven't written   b haven't been writing   c don't write
2 a 've been starting   b start   c 've started
3 a 's gone   b goes   c 's been going
4 a work   b 've been working   c 've worked
5 a haven't finished   b don't finish   c haven't been finishing
6 a far   b a little   c really
7 a decide   b 've decided   c 've been deciding
8 a fairly   b far   c totally
9 a far   b pretty   c a bit
10 a Do you enjoy   b Have you been enjoying   c Have you enjoyed
11 a a bit   b a lot   c absolutely
12 a pretty   b well   c a lot

2 What can you change?

VOCABULARY
Phrasal Verbs: Changes

1 ⭐⭐ (Circle) the correct options.

1 Max has settled (down) / up well at his new school.

2 I'm really *looking* / *seeing* forward to next weekend.

3 I'm going to sign *up* / *down* for yoga classes.

4 Let's *try* / *do* out the new skate park.

5 I'm *having* / *going* through a hard time at the moment.

6 Are you going to turn *up* / *down* Juan's invitation?

2 ⭐⭐ Complete the sentences with the phrasal verbs in the box.

| do without   end up   go back |
| move out   ~~sign up~~   turn out |

1 Did you _____sign up_____ for the school trip to San Diego?

2 The party didn't _____ very well in the end. Not many people came.

3 My sister wants to _____ and be more independent.

4 If you don't work hard at school, you probably won't _____ with a good job.

5 I don't think I could _____ chocolate! I love it!

6 I probably won't _____ to my hometown when I finish college.

3 ⭐⭐⭐ Complete the personality quiz with the correct form of the verbs in the box and the correct prepositions.

| do   go   look forward   ~~move~~   move   sign   try   turn |

Are You a Positive Person?

1 Would you like to *move out* of your family's home before you're 25?

2 In your life, do things usually _____ well?

3 When you are _____ a hard time, do you look for solutions?

4 Do you _____ for a lot of optional activities at school?

5 Do you like to _____ new ways of doing things?

6 When you get up, do you always _____ everything you will do in the day?

7 Would you like to _____ a new country?

8 Could you _____ the Internet for a week?

4 ⭐ Answer *Yes* or *No* to the questions from Exercise 3. How positive are you?

7–8 *yes* answers: very positive!

5–6 *yes* answers: fairly positive!

Less than 5 *yes* answers: not very positive!

5 ⭐⭐⭐ Write four sentences with phrasal verbs about what kind of person you are. (See the *Learn to Learn* tip in the Student's Book, p23.)

_____

_____

_____

_____

Explore It! 🖱

Guess the correct answer.

What is the minimum age when you can start working in the U.S.A. without your parents' permission?

a 14   b 16   c 18

Find an interesting fact about when you can legally do something for the first time in your country. Write a question and send it to a classmate in an email, or ask them in the next class.

READING
A Blog Entry

1 ⭐ Look at the blog entry quickly. Why is Chloe's life new? Mark (✓) the correct answer.

a She's just gotten married. ☐

b She's in college now. ☐

c She's just finished college. ☐

2 ⭐⭐ Read the blog entry and check the meaning of the words in the box in a dictionary. Then complete the sentences.

> ~~disappointed~~   into   law   lecture
> plenty of   surrounded

1 I did badly on my exams. I'm really
 disappointed !

2 I'm really _____ comic books. They're my favorite thing to read.

3 The campsite was _____ by trees, so it was very beautiful.

4 My cousin's studying _____ . He says it's a lot of work.

5 I know _____ people, but do I have any real friends?

6 I've just been to a really interesting _____ .

3 ⭐⭐ Read the first paragraph of the blog entry and answer the questions. Write "no information" if there is no answer in the text.

1 Which college does Chloe go to?
_____

2 What does Chloe mean when she says that you "have to start from zero"?
_____

3 Why are things turning out well?
_____

4 ⭐⭐ Read the second paragraph of the blog entry and complete the chart.

	Studying in High School	Studying in College
1	classes in small groups	
2		
3		

5 ⭐⭐⭐ Do you think it's a good idea to study away from home? Write three or four sentences.

_____
_____
_____
_____
_____

● ● ●

CHLOE'S CORNER   **BLOG**   **ABOUT**   **FAQS**

A NEW LIFE!

Have you ever had a really special time in your life? Well, I'm having one now because I've just started college! I was really looking forward to it, and so far, I haven't been disappointed! My biggest worry before coming was: would it be easy to make new friends? It's a good question because when you go to college, you have to start from zero. The old friends you used to see at home aren't there anymore, so you need to create a completely new social life. Well, I'm glad to say that things are turning out really well. I'm living in a dorm, which is a special building just for students. It's the ideal place to be during your first year because you're surrounded by new faces! And everyone's into making new friends.

Studying in college feels very different from how things used to be in high school. Although there were a lot of students in my high school, there are over 100 students in my lectures now! In high school, we would have the chance to ask questions and discuss things with our teachers. Now you just sit down and take notes! Another big difference is that I only have 12 hours of lectures per week (I'm studying law). The rest of the time I spend studying alone. That can be pretty difficult because you need a lot of discipline! And there are plenty of other, more interesting things to do!

I've settled down really well into college life. There's just one "small" problem: I need to study more!

GRAMMAR IN ACTION

Used To, *Would*, and Simple Past

1 ⭐⭐ **Complete the sentences with the correct form of *used to* and the verbs in parentheses.**

1 I _____used to hate_____ (hate) going to the dentist.

2 My dad _____ (have) more hair.

3 I _____ (not like) carrots.

4 My mom _____ (not go) to the gym.

5 _____ (you / play) the violin?

6 _____ (Matt / be) your best friend?

2 ⭐⭐ **Rewrite the sentences with *used to* when it is possible.**

1 I went to bed at ten o'clock last night.

   not possible

2 In the past, did your grandpa ride a bike to work?

   _____

3 People went to the movies more often before the Internet.

   _____

4 Clothes didn't wear out so quickly before.

   _____

5 Oh, no! Did you leave the keys at home?

   _____

6 Was there a castle in this town before?

   _____

3 ⭐⭐⭐ **Write four sentences about what people *used to* and *didn't use to* do. Use the photos for ideas.**

1 _____

2 _____

3 _____

4 _____

4 ⭐ **Circle the correct options.**

Things Were Different When I Was Young!

Children [1]*would* / *wouldn't* listen to their parents and teachers. Now they don't listen!

People [2]*would* / *wouldn't* run everywhere. They had more time.

We [3]*would* / *wouldn't* play in the street. It wasn't dangerous then.

People [4]*would* / *wouldn't* think about money all the time. They had better values.

Families [5]*would* / *wouldn't* go to another country on vacation. And some families didn't go anywhere!

We [6]*would* / *wouldn't* listen to the radio more because not everyone had a TV.

5 ⭐⭐ **Rewrite the underlined part of the sentences with *would*. If it isn't possible, rewrite the sentences with *used to*.**

1 <u>We lived</u> in the country before.

   We used to live in the country.

2 <u>I often arrived</u> late to school when I was younger.

   _____

3 <u>Did you wear</u> glasses before?

   _____

4 <u>My grandma always went</u> for a walk after breakfast.

   _____

5 <u>My dad often swam</u> in the ocean when he lived in Salvador.

   _____

6 <u>My mom was</u> a nurse before.

   _____

6 ⭐⭐ **Circle the correct option OR options.**

A [1]*Did you take* / *Did you use to take* tennis lessons?

B Yes, I did.

A So, why [2]*did* / *would* you stop?

B My teacher [3]*would* / *used to* criticize me all the time. So one day I [4]*decided* / *used to decide*, "No more tennis lessons!"

A Really? I [5]*didn't* / *didn't use to* know anything about that! Who [6]*did you* / *did you use to* take lessons with?

B My dad!

VOCABULARY AND LISTENING
Parts of Objects

1 ⭐ **Find nine more parts of objects in the word search.**

B	O	L	S	L	E	N	S
H	B	U	T	T	O	N	D
A	C	O	R	D	O	W	P
N	R	C	A	B	O	E	L
D	I	M	P	Z	A	Y	U
L	L	C	O	V	E	R	G
E	I	H	K	E	Y	O	U
T	D	I	S	P	L	A	Y

2 ⭐⭐ **Complete the sentences with words from Exercise 1.**

1 Oh, no! A __strap__ on my backpack has broken.

2 There's a problem with the _____ on my phone. It's very dark.

3 These photos have turned out badly because the _____ on my camera was dirty.

4 Let's carry this bag together. You take one _____ and I'll take the other.

5 Where's the _____ for the saucepan?

6 Is this the _____ for charging your phone?

7 This _____ on my laptop is for changing the audio volume.

8 The _____ of this book looks really great, but the book wasn't very interesting!

9 You need to attach this _____ to the printer.

3 ⭐⭐⭐ **Write a description of a "mystery object." Use at least four of the words from Exercise 1. Send your description in an email to a classmate, or ask them to guess the object in the next class.**

It has a display and it has one or two buttons, but it doesn't have a plug. It doesn't have a handle, but it has a strap. What is it?

_____

_____

_____

_____

A Conversation

🎧 2.01 **4** ⭐ **Listen to a conversation about the past between Katie and her grandma. Mark (✓) the things they mention.**

1 a plug ✓ 2 a calculator ☐

3 a video cassette ☐ 4 a TV ☐

5 a camera ☐ 6 a PowerPoint presentation ☐

5 ⭐ <u>Underline</u> **the key words in the sentences. (See the *Learn to Learn* tip in the Student's Book, p26.)**

1 Katie is going to <u>work on a history project</u>. F

2 Her grandma thinks that young people spend too much time using "technological things." ___

3 Katie's grandma didn't use a calculator in school. ___

4 There weren't many shows on TV before. ___

5 Katie thinks that life before sounds fun. ___

6 When her grandma was in school, each student had a small blackboard to write on. ___

🎧 2.01 **6** ⭐⭐ **Listen again. Are the sentences in Exercise 5 *T* (true) or *F* (false)?**

7 ⭐⭐⭐ **What three modern inventions could you not do without?**

_____

_____

GRAMMAR IN ACTION
Past Perfect with *Never, Ever, Already, By (Then), By the Time*

1 ⭐ **Read the sentences and <u>underline</u> the action that happened first.**

1 I <u>had already had lunch</u> when my sister arrived.

2 My sister had already gotten married by the time she was 20.

3 Dan wasn't happy because I had turned down his invitation.

4 By the time the game ended, we had scored five goals!

5 We had walked a very long way by the time we found the river.

2 ⭐⭐ **Match the beginnings of the sentences (1–5) with the ends (a–e).**

1 I had never seen snow   [c]

2 We had only been at the hotel a few minutes when   ☐

3 Had you ever run more than 5 km   ☐

4 By the time my grandpa settled in the U.S.A.,   ☐

5 We had already been to six different stores   ☐

a by the time Clara decided to buy something.

b before today?

c before I went to Sierra Nevada.

d he'd lived in six different countries.

e the storm started.

3 ⭐⭐ **Put the words in the correct order to make sentences.**

1 car / seen / had / the / already / .
I *had already seen the car.*

2 had / then / back / by / come / .
Jack _____

3 called / woken up / you / I / when / already / ?
Had _____
_____

4 Europe / never / year / had / last / been / I / to / .
Before _____

5 then / a snake / ever / you / before / seen / ?
Had _____
_____

4 ⭐⭐ **Complete the sentences with the simple past or the past perfect form of the verbs in parentheses.**

1 Pablo _had never taken_ (never / take) guitar lessons before he _____gave_____ (give) his first concert.

2 _____ (Sean / ever make) lasagna before yesterday?

3 School _____ (already / start) when I _____ (arrive).

4 By the time Sara _____ (leave) England, she _____ (learn) to speak English very well.

5 I _____ (never / feel) real terror until I _____ (see) that movie!

6 _____ (everyone / already / go) to bed by the time the fire _____ (start)?

5 ⭐⭐⭐ **Complete the text with the simple past or the past perfect form of the verbs in parentheses.**

Emma [1] _____moved_____ (move) to a new school last year. By the time she [2] _____ (be) there a couple of weeks, she [3] _____ (already / settle) down very well. And now things are going even better! Last week, she [4] _____ (become) the captain of the school soccer team.

She [5] _____ (be) very happy about this because she [6] _____ (always / want) to be the team captain. And yesterday she [7] _____ (receive) her exam results. More good news! She [8] _____ (never / get) such good grades before!

6 ⭐⭐⭐ **Complete the sentences with your own ideas. Use the past perfect.**

1 Before this year, I _____

2 We didn't win the game because we _____
_____

3 I signed up for karate lessons because _____
_____

4 By the time Ella finished college, _____
_____

5 Alan was going through a hard time because _____
_____

WRITING
An Opinion Essay

1 ⭐ **Look at the essay quickly. Does the writer think that life used to be better in the past?**

_____

2 ⭐⭐ **Read the essay and answer the questions. Mark (✓) and circle the correct answers.**

1 In which TWO paragraphs does the writer give ideas to support their opinion?

A ☐   B ☐   C ☐   D ☐

2 In paragraph A, the writer ...
  a asks the reader a question.
  b gives their opinion.

3 In paragraph D, the writer ...
  a repeats their opinion.
  b asks the reader a question.

3 ⭐⭐ **Complete the essay with the Useful Language phrases in the box.**

> ~~first~~   in addition   in conclusion
> second   therefore
> this means that

4 ⭐⭐ **What different words or phrases does the writer use to avoid repeating items 1–4 below?**

1 in the past (paragraph B)

_____

2 better (paragraph B)

_____

3 situation (paragraph B)

_____

4 look at (paragraph D)

_____

5 ⭐⭐ **Complete the sentence.**

In paragraphs B and C, to describe life in the past, the writer uses the simple past, _____ , and _____ .

Did Life Use To Be Better?

A Older people often say that, in the past, life used to be better. However, in my opinion, this is simply not true.

B ¹ _____First_____ , let's look at the situation of women. In the old days, many men (and some women) used to think that a woman's role in life was to be a mother and to do the housework and the cooking. Fortunately, attitudes have changed a lot since then! ² _____ women today are in a much more favorable position.

C ³ _____ , the number of very poor people around the world has decreased significantly in the last 20 or 30 years. ⁴ _____ , healthcare has improved in poor countries. In the past, many children would die when they were still very young in those places. This happens far less often now. ⁵ _____ , we can talk about huge change in two very important areas.

D ⁶ _____ , the world today is a much better place. If we examine the facts, no one would want to go back to "the golden past." This past only exists in some people's imaginations. It never existed in reality.

PLAN

6 ⭐⭐ **Write an opinion essay. Look at the statement. Write down three reasons why you agree or disagree with it.**

> It's more important to speak English today than in the past.

_____

_____

_____

WRITE

7 ⭐⭐⭐ **Write your opinion essay. Remember to include four paragraphs and examples of _used to_, _would_, the simple past, the past perfect, and the _Useful Language_ phrases from Exercise 3.**

CHECK

8 **Do you ...**
- give your opinion?
- give reasons for your opinion?
- summarize your opinion?

VOCABULARY

1 Rewrite the second sentence so that it has a similar meaning to the first. Use the phrasal verbs in the box and any other words you need.

> do without   go back   go through   look forward to   move to   settle down   try out   turn down

1 Let's return to the bus station.

Let's _____ the bus station.

2 I'm very excited about the concert on Saturday.

I'm _____ the concert on Saturday.

3 I have to take a shower every morning.

I can't _____ every morning.

4 I'm sorry, but I can't accept your invitation.

I'm sorry, but I have to _____ .

5 Mike's adapting well to life in Milan.

Mike's _____ in Milan.

6 Beth isn't enjoying life at all right now.

Beth is _____ a hard time right now.

7 Jose used to live in California, but he went to live in New York.

Jose _____ New York.

8 Let's see what this new video game is like!

Let's _____ video game!

2 Complete the crossword. Use the picture clues.

Down ↓

Across →

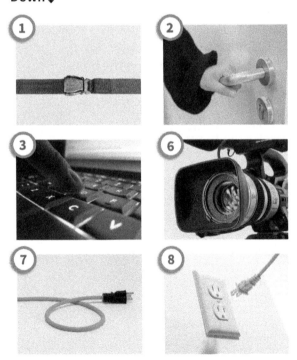

GRAMMAR IN ACTION

3 (Circle) the correct answer.

When my mom was ten, she ¹*got / would get* a cat for her birthday. She ²*would love / loved* the cat, and it used to follow her everywhere. The cat ³*did explore / would explore* other people's yards, and it ⁴*didn't fight / used to fight* with other cats from time to time. Then one day, the cat ⁵*didn't come / used to come* home. Mom ⁶*used to be / was* so sad – she ⁷*put up / would put up* posters to try and find it. Finally, it came home five days later. Mom was very happy!

4 (Circle) the sentence (a or b) that has a similar meaning to the first.

1 The train had already left when we got to the station.
   a When we got to the station, the train left.
   b We arrived at the station late, so we missed the train.

2 Before we went to Brazil last year, I'd never been there.
   a Last year was the first time I was in Brazil.
   b I didn't visit Brazil last year.

3 By the time I learned to drive, I'd spent a lot of money on driving lessons.
   a I spent a lot of money before I could drive.
   b I learned to drive before I spent a lot of money.

4 Amy hadn't finished her homework when Aidan came.
   a Aidan arrived and Amy finished her homework.
   b When Aidan came, Amy was still doing her homework.

5 Ryan had never seen a lion before he went to the zoo last week.
   a Ryan didn't see a lion at the zoo.
   b Before his trip to the zoo last week, Ryan hadn't seen a lion.

6 We had taken a lot of photos by the time our vacation was over.
   a We took a lot of photos on vacation.
   b When our vacation ended, we took a lot of photos.

CUMULATIVE GRAMMAR

5 Complete the text with the missing words. (Circle) the correct options.

Joe said, "I ¹_____ to this new school a month ago, but I ²_____ down to life here very well."
"³_____ through a hard time?" I asked him.
"Yes, I ⁴_____," he said. "It's been ⁵_____ difficult. At my old school I ⁶_____ a lot of friends.
And I ⁷_____ them very often after school. Before I came here, I ⁸_____ that it would be so hard to make new friends.
It's been ⁹_____ harder than I thought."
"¹⁰_____ up for any school clubs?" I asked.
"Yes, I ¹¹_____ to two or three different ones," Joe replied. "You know, I ¹²_____ really popular at my old school," he continued. "Nothing like this ¹³_____ to me before."

1 a moved
  b had moved
  c used to move

2 a didn't settle
  b haven't settled
  c hadn't settled

3 a Did you go
  b Had you gone
  c Have you been going

4 a did
  b have
  c been

5 a far
  b absolutely
  c really

6 a would have
  b used to have
  c have had

7 a had seen
  b have been seeing
  c would see

8 a hadn't expected
  b haven't expected
  c wouldn't expect

9 a pretty
  b totally
  c far

10 a Did you sign
   b Have you signed
   c Had you signed

11 a 've been going
   b had gone
   c would go

12 a used to be
   b would be
   c 've been

13 a had happened
   b has happened
   c has been happening

3 What's usually on your plate?

VOCABULARY
Cooking Verbs

1 ⭐ **Find 11 more verbs for cooking in the word search.**

```
C  H  O  P  O (P  E  E  L)
R  O  V  G  R  I  L  L  D
I  S  E  A  S  O  N  S  I
S  P  R  E  A  D  O  L  B
H  O  C  R  A  M  F  I  O
A  R  O  A  S  T  F  C  I
R  E  O  V  E  R  R  E  L
B  A  K  E  M  Y  Y  O  T
O  M  U  G  R  A  T  E  E
```

2 ⭐ Circle **the verb that goes with the food.**

1 grate / peel cheese
2 bake / boil water
3 peel / season an apple
4 grate / roast a chicken
5 spread / roast butter
6 chop / slice bread
7 grate / fry eggs
8 peel / overcook fish

3 ⭐⭐ **Complete the sentences with the words in the box.**

bake   chop   grill   ~~overcook~~   season   spread

1 Please don't _overcook_ the meat. One or two minutes is enough.
2 _____ the onions into small pieces.
3 Do you often _____ bread in the oven?
4 When you barbecue, you _____ meat over a fire.
5 _____ the dish with salt and pepper.
6 Do you have a knife to _____ the jam?

4 ⭐⭐ **Complete the recipe with the words in the box.**

fry   grate   overcook
season   ~~slice~~   spread

A Fantastic Snack

¹ _Slice_ some bread and toast it. Take some refried beans and ² _____ them on the bread. ³ _____ some cheese and put it on the refried beans. In a pan, heat up some oil. Then put an egg in the pan and ⁴ _____ it for only one or two minutes. Don't ⁵ _____ it! Put the egg on the bread. ⁶ _____ with black pepper. It's ready to eat!

5 ⭐⭐⭐ **Write how to make something simple (e.g., an omelet, a milkshake, your favorite sandwich).**

_____
_____
_____
_____

6 ⭐⭐ **Write the adjective form of the verbs from Exercise 1. (See the** Learn to Learn **tip in the Student's Book, p35.)**

Add -ed	Add -d	Irregular
peeled		

Explore It! 🖱

Guess the correct answer.

What is the main ingredient of this dish called Bombay Duck?

a duck   b horse meat   c fish

Find another interesting fact about food or a special dish. Write a question and send it to a classmate in an email, or ask them in the next class.

READING
An Online Forum

1 ⭐ Match the photos 1–4 with the four comments on the online forum A–D.

2 ⭐⭐ Complete the article with the missing sentence parts a–f.

  a The food was OK

  b and they read some poems

  c because it's so incredibly beautiful

  d My sister doesn't eat meat

  e ~~The highlight of the trip was when we went to an underwater restaurant~~

  f in the summer

3 ⭐⭐ Read the text and check the meaning of the words in the box in a dictionary. Then complete the sentences.

> ~~costume~~ freezing highlight
> hiking melt practical

  1 What _costume_ are you going to wear in the school play?

  2 Riding your bike at night without lights is not _____ at all.

  3 Eat your ice cream quickly or it'll _____!

  4 My friend Mia goes _____ even in the middle of winter!

  5 It's _____ outside, so put on a warm coat.

  6 The _____ of the meal was when they brought out my birthday cake.

4 ⭐⭐⭐ Which of the four places would you most like to eat at? Why? Write three or four sentences.

_____

_____

_____

_____

_____

_____

ASK IT!
HOME ANSWER NOTIFICATIONS SEARCH

Where's the most memorable place you've ever eaten?

A

My dad won $100,000 in the lottery, and he decided to do something very practical with it: he took all of us on vacation to the Maldive Islands! (They're about 640 kilometers southwest of India.) ¹ _e_ . Beautiful tropical fish swam past as we ate! It was an experience that I'll never forget! ² _____ but nothing special.

Sam, Toronto

B

In northern Finland, there's a fantastic snow hotel with a restaurant made of ice! It's only open in the winter. Perhaps it melts ³ _____! You need to wear warm clothes or you're going to be freezing because you sit on ice chairs all the time! We had grilled salmon (very good!), but the roasted meat for the main course was a bit overcooked. Oh, well, nowhere's perfect!

Oona, Helsinki

C

When we were on vacation in Ireland, we went for a medieval dinner at Bunratty Castle. It was a lot of fun! They had actors in traditional costumes, ⁴ _____. There was also Irish music. The food was good, but we didn't eat with our hands like in medieval times! They had vegetarian food, too. ⁵ _____ and she loved the baked carrots with grated cheese.

Charlotte, Denver

D

The most memorable place I've eaten was Pulpit Rock in Norway. The meal wasn't exactly spectacular – a sandwich, an energy bar, and an apple! But the view *was* spectacular! You could see for miles! And the food didn't taste bad after hiking for a couple of hours! It's not easy to get to Pulpit Rock from Ireland. But I might go back a second time ⁶ _____!

Conor, Dublin

GRAMMAR IN ACTION
Future Forms

1 ⭐ **Match the verbs in sentences 1–6 with the uses a–c.**

1 We're meeting at six o'clock. `c`
2 The bus leaves at 10 a.m. ☐
3 I'm going to study more this year. ☐
4 Are you and Luis playing tennis tonight? ☐
5 The restaurant opens at 7 p.m. ☐
6 Zoe's going to try to make lasagna. ☐

a to talk about future plans and intentions
b to talk about scheduled or timetabled events
c to talk about fixed arrangements in the future

2 ⭐⭐ (Circle) **the correct options.**

1 What *do you do* / *(are you doing)* tonight?
2 The game *starts* / *is starting* in five minutes!
3 My sister *learns* / *is going to learn* to drive next year.
4 We *meet* / *'re meeting* in the park at six o'clock.
5 I *make* / *'m going to make* dinner in a few minutes.
6 Joel *has* / *is going to have* a piano lesson in a few minutes.
7 I *'m getting* / *'m going to get* my green belt in judo this year. It's my big goal for the year.
8 We *go* / *'re going* skateboarding this weekend.

3 ⭐⭐⭐ **Write about two fixed future arrangements that you have or haven't made and two future intentions that you have or don't have.**

_____
_____
_____
_____

4 ⭐ **Match the underlined verbs in sentences 1–3 with the uses a–c.**

1 Those cookies smell amazing. And I'm sure <u>they're going to taste</u> delicious! ☐
2 More people <u>will become</u> vegetarians in the future. ☐
3 I <u>might want</u> some more pizza. Let me finish this first! ☐

a a future prediction that we don't feel sure about
b a future prediction based on evidence in the present
c a future prediction that we feel sure about

5 ⭐⭐ **Complete the predictions with** *be going to*, *will*, **or** *may*/*might*, **and the verbs in the box.**

| come   have   love   ~~miss~~   not cost   not finish |

1 Oh, no! It's 5:59! We ___'re going to miss___ the six o'clock train!
2 John _____ to the party. Let's wait and see!
3 I'm sure Deborah _____ the present you chose for her. You have great taste.
4 This meal _____ a lot! Prices are cheap!
5 Some experts say that one day everyone in the world _____ enough food to eat.
6 I _____ this book tonight, but I'm going to try.

6 ⭐⭐⭐ **Complete the conversation with the correct form of the verbs in parentheses. Use the simple present, present continuous,** *be going to*, *will*, **or** *may*/*might*.

A I ¹___'m never going to cook___ (never / cook) a big meal again!
B Why? It wasn't so bad. And I'm sure your cooking ²_____ (get) better in the future.
A Hmm … I suppose I ³_____ (make) some progress.
B Don't be so negative! Anyway, what ⁴_____ (you / do) after lunch?
A I ⁵_____ (go) to the movies with Will. The movie ⁶_____ (start) at 5 p.m.

7 ⭐⭐⭐ **Complete the sentences with your own ideas.**

1 In ten years, I might _____
_____.
2 In 100 years, everyone will _____
_____.
3 I might _____
_____.

VOCABULARY AND LISTENING
Quantities

1 ⭐ (Circle) the correct quantity to describe each photo.

1 (a splash) / cup of milk

2 a bag / pinch of salt

3 a spoonful / bag of sugar

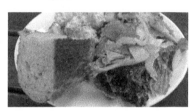

4 a slice / piece of bread

5 a sprinkle / handful of sugar

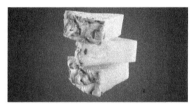

6 cups / chunks of pineapple

2 ⭐⭐ Complete the chart with the quantities in the box. (See the *Learn to Learn* tip in the Student's Book, p38.)

> a bag of   a cup of   a handful of   a piece of
> a pinch of   a slice of   a splash of   a spoonful of
> a sprinkle of   ~~chunks of~~

Sugar	Milk	Cheese
		chunks of

3 ⭐⭐⭐ Write about three things you like to eat or drink. Use the quantities from Exercise 2.

I love two slices of toast and jam for breakfast.

_____

_____

An Interview

🎧 **4** ⭐ Listen to a man talking about his job. Are the sentences *T* (true) or *F* (false)?
3.01

1 James has his own food store. ___
2 James works a lot. ___
3 His job has several good points. ___
4 He never has time to eat the food that he cooks. ___

🎧 **5** ⭐⭐⭐ Listen again and complete the sentences with ONE word from the interview.
3.01

1 James works in the city of _Chicago_ .
2 In the restaurant, there can be _____ people eating at the same time.
3 The food needs to arrive at customers' tables quickly and the dishes need to be of _____ quality.
4 James doesn't _____ down very often while he's working.
5 It's a profession for people who are _____ .
6 It's very different from an _____ job.
7 The opinion of the _____ is important to James.
8 It's important to _____ the food.

6 ⭐⭐⭐ Would you like to do James' job? Why / Why not? Write three or four sentences.

_____

_____

_____

_____

_____

_____

GRAMMAR IN ACTION
Future Continuous and Future Perfect

1 ⭐ **Complete the sentences with the verbs in parentheses in the future continuous.**

1 I _____'ll be reading_____ (read) this book all evening.

2 He _____ (listen) to the podcast later.

3 I _____ (not lie) on the sofa all afternoon!

4 My parents _____ (not work) this time tomorrow.

5 _____ (we / eat) at two o'clock?

6 _____ (Ryan / cook) for a long time?

2 ⭐⭐ **Look at Carmen's diary. Complete the sentences with the correct future continuous form of the verbs in parentheses and short or long answers.**

Monday	Tuesday	Wednesday
tennis (5 p.m.)	homework (morning)	dance class (6 p.m.)

1 She _____'ll be playing_____ (play) tennis at 5 p.m. on Monday.

2 She _____ (not do) homework on Tuesday afternoon.

3 She _____ (start) her dance class at 6 p.m. on Wednesday.

4 A _____ (Carmen / play tennis) on Monday?

  B _____

5 A What day _____ (she / take) her dance class?

  B _____

3 ⭐ (Circle) **the correct options.**

1 I'm going to bed very late tonight. I *'ll* / (*won't*) have gone to bed by 11 p.m.

2 I hope that I *'ll* / *won't* have learned to drive in a few years. I think it would be fantastic!

3 My mom works in another country. By tomorrow, I *'ll* / *won't* have seen her for two months.

4 My dad often cooks for the family. He *'ll* / *won't* have cooked several meals for us by the end of this week.

5 A Will you have become a doctor by the time you're 20?

  B That's impossible! *Yes, I will.* / *No, I won't.*

4 ⭐⭐ **Complete the conversation with the verbs in the box in the future perfect and short answers.**

> arrive   grill   ~~make~~   not fry   not have   slice

A ¹_____Will_____ you _____have made_____ lunch by one o'clock?

B No, ²_____. Why?

A The guests ³_____ by then!

B Oh, no! I ⁴_____ the potatoes to make the fries, but I ⁵_____ them.

A And ⁶_____ you _____ all the meat?

B No, ⁷_____. I ⁸_____ time!

5 ⭐⭐ (Circle) **the correct time expression.**

1 I'll be sleeping (*in two hours*) / *since next week*.

2 Will you be sitting by the pool *this time tomorrow* / *since the time you were 18*?

3 We'll have finished all our exams *by the end of this month* / *for three hours*!

4 *Next Tuesday* / *By the end of this year*, we'll have visited five different countries!

5 We'll be eating that roasted chicken *in five minutes* / *by the time it's cooked*.

6 ⭐⭐⭐ **Use the future continuous or future perfect to write about things that you will do or hope that you will do.**

1 By the end of this year, _____.

2 At nine o'clock tonight, _____.

3 Next weekend, _____.

4 By the time I'm 30, _____.

WRITING
A Listicle

1 ⭐ Look at the listicle quickly. What is it about?

_____

2 ⭐⭐ Read the listicle. Are the sentences *T* (true) or *F* (false)?

1 Tight clothes will be popular. _F_

2 We will need to buy new clothes more often. ____

3 We will wear very different shoes from today. ____

4 We'll have less choice when we buy clothes. ____

5 Clothes will become intelligent. ____

3 ⭐⭐⭐ Rewrite the sentences with the underlined *Useful Language* phrases in the listicle.

1 More information here soon!

Watch this space!

_____

2 Smart clothes will be the usual thing we wear.

_____

3 I can't imagine anything more exciting than being a fashion designer.

_____

4 T-shirts will always be popular. *(three expressions)*

_____

_____

FIVE FUTURE FASHION TRENDS!

1 Baggy clothes will be everywhere!

Comfortable baggy clothes <u>will be the norm</u> as the planet gets hotter. Tight denim jeans will have gone completely out of style by 2030, and clothes made of cool cotton will be in all the stores.

2 Clothes will wear out more quickly!

Fast fashion will mean that most clothes will only last five or six months. Clothes will become cheaper as a result.

3 Sneakers <u>are here to stay</u>!

People of all ages wear sneakers nowadays, and that isn't going to change. If you ask me, sneakers <u>will be around forever</u>. I love sneakers, so <u>what could be better</u> news than that?

4 Clothes to match eyes and hair color!

Very soon, we won't just be buying clothes by size. You'll be able to buy clothes to match your eyes or hair color. Everything will be personalized. <u>Watch this space!</u>

5 High-tech clothes!

We already have smartphones, and they <u>aren't going anywhere</u>. But soon we'll have smart clothes, too! They'll adapt to our body temperature and even to our size! The future's going to be exciting!

PLAN

4 ⭐⭐ Write your own listicle. Take notes in your notebook on the theme "Five ways my life will be different in 20 years." Use the spidergram to generate ideas.

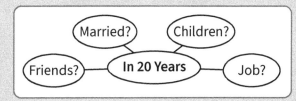

WRITE

5 ⭐⭐⭐ Write your listicle. Remember to include future forms, vocabulary from this unit, and phrases from the *Useful Language* box (see Student's Book, p41).

CHECK

6 Do you ...
- explain what you will or might be doing in the future?
- explain what will be normal in the future?
- make any other predictions?

VOCABULARY

1 Complete the crossword. Use the clues.

ACROSS →

4 _____ an egg
5 _____ an apple
6 _____ bread
7 _____ chicken
9 _____ a cake
11 _____ sausages

DOWN ↓

1 _____ onions
2 _____ a veggie burger
3 _____ cheese
6 _____ meat
8 _____ butter
10 _____ water

2 Circle the correct options.

1 a cup of *sugar / fish*
2 a piece of *salt / chocolate*
3 a slice of *cake / milk*
4 some chunks of *yogurt / cheese*
5 a handful of *nuts / milk*
6 a bag of *water / chips*
7 a pinch of *pepper / chicken*
8 a sprinkle of *potatoes / grated cheese*
9 a spoonful of *apples / olive oil*
10 a splash of *vinegar / salt*

GRAMMAR IN ACTION

3 Circle the correct options.

1 What time *does / will* the movie start?
2 I *will / 'm going to* make pizza for the first time next weekend.
3 *Do you go / Are you going* to the market with Sean this weekend?
4 Dad *might / will* be late for dinner tonight. It depends on when he finishes work.
5 I think that in the future people *will eat / are eating* less meat.
6 My cousin *will stay / is staying* at my house tonight.

4 Complete the predictions with the future perfect or future continuous form of the verbs in parentheses.

Space Predictions

- In 20 years, scientists [1]_____ (discover) a new planet in our solar system.
- People [2]_____ (live) on Mars by the end of this century.
- A big asteroid [3]_____ (not hit) the Earth by the end of this millennium.
- People [4]_____ (go) to the moon for their vacations in 50 years.
- We [5]_____ (not find) intelligent life in the rest of the universe by the end of this century.
- Scientists [6]_____ (plan) journeys outside the solar system very soon.

5 Complete the text with the missing words. (Circle) the correct options.

Then

Now

The Future

Teen Fashion: Past, Present, and Future

Teenagers ¹_____ clothes especially designed for them for long. Before the 1950s, they ²_____ their own fashion, and clothing companies ³_____ about making special clothes for them. In the past, young teenagers ⁴_____ children's clothes, and teenagers that were ⁵_____ older wore adults' clothes. Clothes for teenagers ⁶_____ a lot since then! It's ⁷_____ hard to predict what kind of clothes teenagers ⁸_____ in the future because fashion changes very quickly. They ⁹_____ wear high-tech clothes, or perhaps they ¹⁰_____ 1960s hippie-style clothes soon. Who knows? Two things are ¹¹_____ clear, though – fashion designers ¹²_____ very good at inventing new teen styles in the past, and they ¹³_____ to continue doing this in the future, too.

1 a weren't wearing	b haven't been wearing	c haven't worn
2 a didn't use to have	b wouldn't have	c weren't having
3 a have never thought	b would never think	c had never thought
4 a have been wearing	b would wear	c were wearing
5 a a bit	b really	c a far
6 a had changed	b have changed	c have been changing
7 a extremely	b a lot	c absolutely
8 a are wearing	b will have worn	c will be wearing
9 a will	b might	c 're going to
10 a wear	b 're wearing	c 'll be wearing
11 a pretty	b a lot	c far
12 a are	b have been	c had been
13 a are trying	b will have tried	c are going to try

4 How do you use your senses?

VOCABULARY
The Five Senses

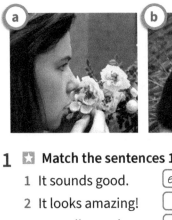 a
 b
 c
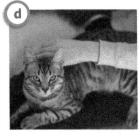 d
 e

1 ⭐ **Match the sentences 1–5 with the pictures a–e.**

1 It sounds good. [e]
2 It looks amazing! [ ]
3 It smells good. [ ]
4 It feels nice. [ ]
5 It tastes great. [ ]

2 ⭐⭐ **Complete the sentences with the correct form of** *feel,* *look, smell, sound,* **or** *taste,* **and** *like* **if necessary.**

1 That song _____sounds_____ good. Who is it?

2 I love this ice cream. It _____ fantastic!

3 You _____ a movie star in those sunglasses!

4 Can you give me a massage? Oh, that _____ so good!

5 Please open the window. It doesn't _____ good in here!

6 Do I _____ an American when I speak English?

7 This bread _____ cardboard! It's very dry!

8 The sky _____ dark. I think it's going to rain.

3 ⭐⭐ **Complete the chart with your own ideas. Write three things for each column. (See the** *Learn to Learn* **tip in the Student's Book, p47.)**

It Feels Good	It Looks Good	It Smells Good	It Sounds Good	It Tastes Good
a cat's fur				

4 ⭐⭐⭐ **Write four sentences about what you experienced with your senses yesterday. Use** *feel, look, smell, sound,* **or** *taste,* **and** *like* **if necessary.**

My new shoes looked good.

_____

_____

_____

_____

_____

_____

_____

_____

Explore It! 🖱

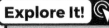

Guess the correct answer.
How far away can elephants smell water?
a 5 km   b 12 km   c 19 km

Find another interesting fact about animal senses. Write a question and send it to a classmate in an email, or ask them in the next class.

For most of us, eating chocolate is a pleasure. But for Alice Schaffer, it's much more than that – it's a full-time job! Alice, you see, works for an important food company, and she eats their chocolate to see how it tastes. Before she worked there, she didn't have a **background** in food science. She was, in fact, working as a salesperson. Then one day, a neighbor told her that her company was looking for people to work as taste-testers. Alice immediately thought, "That sounds like a great job! And I might be good at it because I love chocolate!" So she applied and ... they gave her the job! Of course, it isn't enough to like chocolate if you want to get a job tasting chocolate. You need to be able to identify and **accurately** describe different **flavors** and textures. And that's something you can't learn – you're either born with it or you aren't.

When Alice tells people what she **does for a living**, they often look surprised because they imagine that she must spend all day eating chocolate. But her job isn't really like that at all. When she tastes the chocolate from a bar, she just eats a little piece. You don't need to eat the whole bar to know what it tastes like! The hardest part of the job is when she tastes something that isn't 100 percent right. The **challenge** is to describe exactly what's wrong with the taste. The food technicians need this precise information so they can investigate the problem.

Alice is extremely **proud** of her job, and it's easy to see why: there can't be many people in the world whose job helps give so much pleasure to others!

READING
A Magazine Article

1 ⭐ **Read the magazine article quickly. What is Alice Schaffer's job?**

a She makes chocolate.

b She checks the taste of chocolate.

c She sells chocolate.

2 ⭐⭐ **Match the words in bold in the article with the definitions.**

1 feeling pleasure because you've done something well
_____proud_____

2 particular tastes
_____

3 someone's past situation
_____

4 correctly, without making any mistakes
_____

5 does to earn money
_____

6 something that needs effort or might be hard to do
_____

3 ⭐⭐ **Read the text again. For each question, circle the correct option.**

1 What is the writer trying to do in this article?

a explain how to get a job as a chocolate taster

b write a biography of Alice Schaffer

c describe what a chocolate taster does

(d) tell the reader about the professional life of Alice Schaffer

2 What kind of useful experience had Alice had before?

a She had worked as a salesperson.

b She had studied food science.

c She hadn't really had any experience.

d Her neighbor had taught her about the job.

3 What is the principal quality you need to be a chocolate taster?

a dedication   b natural talent   c to love chocolate   d to write very well

4 What is the most difficult part of the job?

a giving precise information when the quality isn't good

c people not thinking it's a serious job

b not eating the chocolate

d working with the food technicians

5 What might Alice say to a friend about her job?

a It's an easy job.

c There's often a lot of stress in my job.

b I love my job!

d The chocolate is bad for me.

4 ⭐⭐⭐ **Would you like to do Alice Schaffer's job? Why / Why not?**

_____
_____

GRAMMAR IN ACTION
Modals of Deduction and Possibility

1 ⭐ **Match the sentences 1–3 with their meanings a–c.**

1 I'm sure it's nice to work as a chocolate taster. ◯
2 Perhaps it's nice to work as a chocolate taster. ◯
3 I'm sure it isn't nice to work as a chocolate taster. ◯

a It can't be nice to work as a chocolate taster.
b It must be nice to work as a chocolate taster.
c It might be nice to work as a chocolate taster.

2 ⭐⭐ **Look at the sentence** *It might be nice to work as a chocolate taster.* **Which two modal verbs can we use in place of** *might,* **without changing the meaning?**

_____

3 ⭐ (Circle) **the correct options to describe the pictures.**

He *can't* /(*must*) be tired.

He *can't* / *must* feel relaxed.

That car *can't* / *must* be expensive!

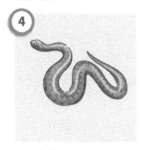
Careful! It *might* / *must* be dangerous.

It *can't* / *must* be raining.

They *may* / *can't* still have some good bargains.

4 ⭐⭐ **Complete the conversation about the photo with** *must, might,* **or** *can't.*

A Look at this photo! What is it?
B It ¹ _might_ be a house!
A No, it ² _____ be! How would you get in?
B It ³ _____ be a fake photo. You never know …
A No, the photo's real. I think it ⁴ _____ be art or something. There ⁵ _____ be another explanation. I'm sure the artist is famous.
B Perhaps … you ⁶ _____ be right. The person who designed it ⁷ _____ be very creative!

5 ⭐⭐⭐ **Rewrite the sentences so that they have the same meaning. Use** *must, might, may, could,* **or** *can't.*

1 Perhaps Nathan's still at school.
   Nathan might/may/could still be at school.
2 I'm sure that isn't the right answer.
   _____
3 I'm sure you need good exam results to study medicine in college.
   _____
4 This is possibly the worst movie I've seen!
   _____
5 I'm sure it doesn't take a long time to make that dish.
   _____

6 ⭐⭐⭐ **Write deductions about these situations. Use** *must, might, could,* **or** *can't.*

1 Edison is a professional soccer player.
   He must be very fit.
2 All the stores are closed.
   _____
3 Your phone isn't working.
   _____
4 Everyone is looking at the sky.

VOCABULARY AND LISTENING
Describing Texture, Sound, Taste, Etc.

1 ⭐ **Complete the adjectives.**

1 spic _y_
2 rou ___
3 shin ___
4 fain ___
5 color _____

6 sou ___
7 smoo ___
8 shar ___
9 smell ___
10 transpar _____

2 ⭐⭐ **Write an appropriate adjective from Exercise 1 before the nouns.**

1 __spicy__ curry
2 dirty, _____ socks
3 nice, _____ skin
4 _____ cream
5 _____, new scissors
6 _____ flowers

3 ⭐⭐ **Complete the sentences with adjectives from Exercise 1.**

1 A crocodile has very __sharp__ teeth.
2 This sauce is too _____ for me. My mouth's burning!
3 Can you pass the sugar? This yogurt is very _____.
4 Does this cake have bananas in it? I can detect a _____ taste of them, but it's not very strong.
5 This lotion is great! My hands feel so _____!
6 This metal box looks very _____ when it's in the sun.
7 Tom's chin felt _____ because he hadn't shaved.

4 ⭐⭐⭐ **Write short descriptions of the items in the box. Use at least one adjective from Exercise 1 in each description. You can use affirmative or negative verbs.**

> apple   cats   my favorite food   snakes

1 _____
2 _____
3 _____
4 _____

An Interview

🎧 5 ⭐ **Listen to an interview about the senses. According to Simon Redding, which of our senses is the most important?**
4.01

a hearing ☐
b sight ☐
c smell ☐
d touch ☐

🎧 6 ⭐⭐ **Listen again. For each question, ⟨circle⟩ the correct option.**
4.01

1 Simon says that some people …
   ⟨a⟩ can't smell very much.
   b use sight and smell well.
   c feel cold all the time.

2 What does Simon say about dreams?
   a Some people open their eyes when they dream.
   b It's good to have colorful images.
   c Taste and smell are not usually part of dreams.

3 When we are communicating, we …
   a shouldn't only be listening.
   b need to smile.
   c shouldn't be negative.

4 What has the biggest impact on us in a conversation?
   a how well the other person listens
   b how the other person moves and looks at us
   c the language that the other person uses

5 What would Simon Redding like people to do?
   a depend on their eyes to understand better
   b remember to use all of their senses
   c close their eyes and feel objects

7 ⭐⭐⭐ **Think about what you have done today. When have you used each of the five senses?**

_____
_____
_____
_____
_____

GRAMMAR IN ACTION
Obligation, Prohibition, Necessity, and Advice

1 ★★ (Circle) the correct options.

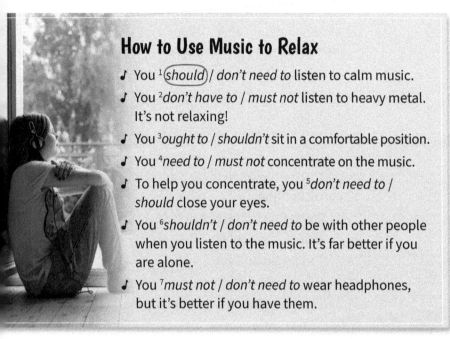

How to Use Music to Relax

♪ You ¹(should) / *don't need to* listen to calm music.

♪ You ²*don't have to* / *must not* listen to heavy metal. It's not relaxing!

♪ You ³*ought to* / *shouldn't* sit in a comfortable position.

♪ You ⁴*need to* / *must not* concentrate on the music.

♪ To help you concentrate, you ⁵*don't need to* / *should* close your eyes.

♪ You ⁶*shouldn't* / *don't need to* be with other people when you listen to the music. It's far better if you are alone.

♪ You ⁷*must not* / *don't need to* wear headphones, but it's better if you have them.

2 ★★ Complete the the interview with a perfume maker with the missing words. (Circle) the correct options.

A ¹_____ study a lot before you became a perfume maker?

B Yes, I ²_____. I ³_____ study chemistry for four years.

A And I suppose that a perfume maker ⁴_____ to have a good sense of smell!

B Yes, of course. You ⁵_____ consider becoming a perfume maker without that! And you ⁶_____ to be very patient because it takes a long time to create the right smell. And you ⁷_____ copy other people. That's bad! You ⁸_____ to be original!

1 a Must you   b Should you   (c) Did you have to
2 a must   b have   c did
3 a had to   b need to   c ought to
4 a must   b should   c needs
5 a should   b shouldn't   c don't have to
6 a must   b need   c don't have
7 a must not   b don't need to   c should
8 a must   b have   c should

3 ★★★ Rewrite the sentences with *must*, *should*, *need*, or *have to*.

1 I recommend that you see a doctor.

   You should see a doctor.

2 It's not permitted to walk on the grass.

   _____

3 There's no obligation for us to watch the game.

   _____

4 Antonio didn't have an obligation to give me a present.

   _____

5 It's necessary for us to contact him.

   _____

6 Being in the sun without a hat is not recommended.

   _____

Past Obligation

4 ★★★ Put the words in the correct order.

1 had / exams / yesterday / two / to / I / take / .

   I had to take two exams yesterday.

2 didn't / have / She / year / walk / last / to / school / to / .

   _____

3 party / had / Miguel / to / so / study, / didn't / the / go / he / to / .

   _____

4 have / people / to / tickets / Did / buy / ?

   _____

WRITING
An Encyclopedia Entry

Marlee Matlin, August 24, 1965

1 Marlee Matlin is an actress. She is the only deaf actress who has won an Oscar.

2 Marlee <u>was born</u> in 1965 and <u>grew up</u> in a small town near Chicago. <u>At the age of</u> 18 months, she lost almost all her hearing. She acted for the first time at the age of seven in a production of *The Wizard of Oz* with actors who were all deaf. In 1986, she won the Oscar for best actress at the age of only 21. In the movie, she didn't have to speak. She played the role of a deaf woman who refuses to speak because the rest of the world refuses to learn sign language.

3 Marlee has appeared in many movies and TV shows, <u>including</u> *Sesame Street*. She isn't just famous as an actress; she is also <u>known as</u> an enthusiastic worker for many charities.

4 Marlee can speak quite well, and she doesn't always need to use an interpreter because she can read people's lips. <u>According to</u> her autobiography, she never planned to become an actress. She thought there wouldn't be any opportunities for deaf people.

---

1 ⭐⭐ Read the encyclopedia entry. What is Marlee's occupation?

_____

2 ⭐⭐ Complete the sentences with information from the encyclopedia entry.

1 She was born _in 1965_ .

2 When she was seven, _____ .

3 In the movie where she won an Oscar, her character was

_____ .

4 She is also famous as _____ .

5 She can read people's lips, so _____ .

6 When she was young, she used to think that

_____ .

3 ⭐⭐ Complete the sentences with the <u>underlined</u> *Useful Language* in the encyclopedia entry.

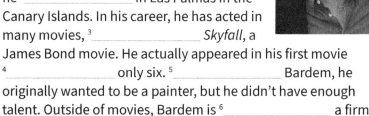

Javier Bardem, March 1, 1969

Javier Bardem [1] _grew up_ in Madrid, but he [2] _____ in Las Palmas in the Canary Islands. In his career, he has acted in many movies, [3] _____ *Skyfall*, a James Bond movie. He actually appeared in his first movie [4] _____ only six. [5] _____ Bardem, he originally wanted to be a painter, but he didn't have enough talent. Outside of movies, Bardem is [6] _____ a firm defender of ecological causes.

PLAN

4 ⭐⭐ Write an encyclopedia entry. First, take notes in your notebook about your favorite actor, fictional character, or athlete.

- Name and date of birth
- A short general description
- Information about their life
- An interesting fact

WRITE

5 ⭐⭐⭐ Write your entry. Remember to include four paragraphs, vocabulary from this unit, and phrases from the *Useful Language* box (see Student's Book, p53).

CHECK

6 Do you ...
- include the person's name and date of birth?
- include information about the person's life?
- include information about the person's work?

VOCABULARY

1 Complete the sentences with the correct form of *feel* (*like*), *look* (*like*), *smell* (*like*), *sound* (*like*), or *taste* (*like*).

1 It doesn't _____ very good in here. Please open the windows.

2 When you sing, you don't really _____ an angel!

3 Wow! That photo _____ a painting! It's so artistic!

4 **A** Do you want to go skateboarding?
  B Yes, that _____ a good idea!

5 This perfume _____ roses and oranges. It's great!

6 It _____ an oven in here! Please turn the air conditioning on!

7 This strawberry ice cream _____ great! Did you make it yourself?

8 These tomatoes _____ really green, and they _____ really hard. So, I don't think they're going to _____ very good!

2 Complete the crossword. Use the clues.

Across →

2 If you have a stomachache, you shouldn't eat _____ food.

3 I love Chinese food, especially sweet and _____ chicken.

4 That bird is very _____. It looks beautiful.

5 The metal buttons on your coat look very _____ under these lights.

6 A rhinoceros has hard, _____ skin.

Down ↓

1 There's a _____ taste of lemon in this cake, but it isn't very strong.

2 That sweater is _____. You need to wash it.

3 I like the feel of this leather. It's very _____.

5 Be careful – it's very _____! Don't cut yourself!

GRAMMAR IN ACTION

3 Complete the conversation with *might*, *must*, or *can't*.

A Is the new *Mission Impossible* movie good?

B I haven't seen it yet, but it [1]_____ be pretty good. It has four stars in the newspaper.

A You never know, it [2]_____ be awful.

B You [3]_____ be serious! They spend a lot of money to make those movies. So, it [4]_____ be fantastic!

A Hmm, you [5]_____ be right. But it [6]_____ be as good as the last one. That's the best movie I've ever seen.

B You [7]_____ be surprised. David's seen it and he couldn't stop talking about it!

A Really? Then it [8]_____ be great! David and I always agree about movies!

4 Complete the sentences with the correct form of *must (not)*, *(not) need to*, *should*, or *(not) have to*.

1 You _____ touch the paintings. It's not allowed!

2 We _____ get up early this morning because the train left at seven o'clock.

3 I don't think you _____ wear green with purple, but it's your decision.

4 I _____ borrow your bike, but thanks for the offer.

5 _____ you _____ wear a uniform at your old school?

6 I _____ clean up my bedroom tonight, but I'm not going to do it.

7 You _____ help me, but it'd be great if you could.

8 _____ we _____ get a visa to travel to Argentina?

CUMULATIVE GRAMMAR

5 Complete the conversation with the missing words. (Circle) the correct options.

CHRIS What ¹_____ this weekend?

TOM I ²_____ any plans yet.

CHRIS What about this new Sensorium exhibition? It ³_____ be good. You never know.

TOM I ⁴_____ to it! It was so interesting that I ⁵_____ about it all the time. It ⁶_____ be the best exhibition I've ever been to. I'm ⁷_____ sure about that. I ⁸_____ that going to museums to look at paintings was boring. But this exhibition is different because you listen to music and smell things while you're looking at each painting. I ⁹_____ that an exhibition could be like that! You ¹⁰_____ go, Chris! You ¹¹_____ disappointed!

CHRIS Thanks! I ¹²_____ miss it! By next Monday, both of us ¹³_____ it!

1 a do you do	b will you do	c are you doing
2 a don't make	b haven't made	c haven't been making
3 a might	b must	c will
4 a 'd already been	b may have been	c 've already been
5 a 've been thinking	b 've thought	c think
6 a can	b needs to	c must
7 a pretty	b absolutely	c far
8 a would think	b used to think	c 've been thinking
9 a 've never imagined	b might never imagine	c 'd never imagined
10 a should	b don't have to	c 'll
11 a can't be	b won't be	c haven't been
12 a won't	b don't need to	c aren't going to
13 a will see	b will have seen	c will be seeing

5 What amazes you?

VOCABULARY
Processes

1 ⭐ Find 11 more verbs in the word search. Write them below. You have the first letter of each verb.

C	O	P	R	O	D	U	C	E	P	Z	C
M	E	A	S	U	R	E	G	V	C	Q	O
E	S	C	S	U	P	P	L	Y	R	M	M
B	R	T	I	D	E	L	I	V	E	R	M
Z	A	R	O	E	Y	U	I	D	A	C	U
N	S	I	C	V	C	O	L	E	T	O	N
C	O	N	N	E	C	T	O	P	E	L	I
H	L	O	T	L	O	I	L	L	O	L	C
T	V	P	G	O	L	B	N	Z	G	E	A
E	E	X	V	P	A	T	T	R	A	C	T
W	Y	G	I	U	V	K	W	A	S	T	E

1 p produce
2 m _____
3 s _____
4 d _____
5 c _____
6 a _____
7 w _____
8 c _____
9 c _____
10 d _____
11 c _____
12 s _____

2 ⭐⭐ Circle the correct options. (See the *Learn to Learn* tip in the Student's Book, p59.)

1 The school supplied us _____ books and other materials for the project.
   a with   b for   c on

2 Flowers attract bees and other insects _____ bright colors and nice smells.
   a about   b with   c at

3 We measured the distance _____ the door to the window.
   a between   b with   c from

3 ⭐⭐ Complete the amazing facts with verbs from Exercise 1.

1 The albatross, a type of seabird, has wings that _measure_ almost 3.5 meters.

2 Some scientists say that trees in forests _____ with each other.

3 One cow can _____ around 12 liters of milk every day.

4 Europeans _____ an average of around 180 kilograms of food every year.

5 The man who _____ pizza to the 2014 Oscars ceremony got a tip of $1,000 from the actors.

6 The UK tea company Twinings has been _____ the British Royal family with tea since 1837.

4 ⭐⭐⭐ Find out some other amazing facts and write sentences about them. Use verbs from Exercise 1.

The tallest building in the world is the Burj Khalifa in Dubai. It measures 828 meters.

_____

_____

_____

_____

_____

_____

Explore It!

True or false?
Cats always land on their feet.

Find another interesting fact about an animal and write a true or false sentence about it. Send it to a classmate in an email, or ask them in the next class.

READING

A Webzine Article

1 ⭐ **Read the article quickly. What color is the aurora borealis normally? In what color has it been seen in southern Europe?**

2 ⭐⭐ **Match the <u>underlined</u> words in the article with the definitions 1–6.**

1 when the sun appears in the sky ____*sunrise*____

2 used physical force to win against someone

____

3 spirits of dead people ____

4 problems or difficulties ____

5 parts of a war, fights between two armies

____

6 the person who makes something ____

3 ⭐⭐ **Read the article again. Are the sentences *T* (true) or *F* (false)? Correct the false sentences.**

1 Aurora, Helios, and Selene were all sisters.

F. Helios was the brother of Aurora and Selene.

2 It is unusual to find a story about the aurora borealis in a culture.

____

3 The French Revolution happened after red lights were seen in the sky over England and Scotland.

____

4 The Cree people in Canada believed the lights were a bad sign.

____

5 The Vikings believed the lights helped lead dead soldiers to their resting place.

____

6 Electrical energy from the sun produces the aurora borealis.

____

4 ⭐⭐⭐ **Write your answer to the question at the end of the article.**

____

____

____

Aurora Borealis: A Wonder of Nature

Origin of the Name

The aurora borealis is an amazing natural light show around the Arctic Circle – a wonder of nature. The name comes from ancient Greek – *aurora* means "<u>sunrise</u>" and *boreas* means "wind." The ancient Greeks believed that Aurora was the sister of Helios (the sun god) and Selene (the moon goddess). As the sun rose in the morning, Aurora flew across the sky to remind her brother and sister that a new day had arrived. Strange stories connected to the lights are found in many cultures.

Europe: Bad Signs

It was strange that the lights, normally green in color, were seen in Greece. Scientists believe that the lights appeared red so far south. In 1789, red lights were seen by the inhabitants of England and Scotland. Shortly after this the French Revolution started, and many believed that the lights had been a sign of the <u>trouble</u> to come.

North America: Other Meanings

The Algonquin people in Canada believed the lights came from a fire that was built by Nanahbozah, their <u>creator</u>. This fire was a sign that Nanahbozah was watching over everyone. Their neighbors, the Cree, on the other hand, thought that the lights were like <u>ghosts</u> who were trying to communicate with the living.

Viking Women

Another ancient civilization – the Vikings – thought the lights were made by the Valkyrie, women who <u>fought</u> in their <u>battles</u>. This light delivered dead soldiers safely to Valhalla, where they could finally rest.

The Scientific Explanation

Now we know that the lights are created by the sun. Sometimes, scientists say, the sun sends huge amounts of electrical energy into space. When this energy reaches Earth, it produces these strange lights in the sky. But which explanation do you prefer?

GRAMMAR IN ACTION
The Passive

1 ⭐ Circle the correct options.

1 This coffee *is* / *are* produced in Kenya – try it.

2 The problem with my computer *was* / *were* solved by turning it off and then on again.

3 In the future, a lot of diseases *are* / *will be* cured with technology.

4 We're going to recycle all the plastic bags so nothing will be *waste* / *wasted*.

5 Some people thought the aurora borealis *is* / *was* created by gods.

6 Was there a loud bang when all the cords *was* / *were* connected?

2 ⭐⭐ Complete the sentences with the correct form of the verbs in the box.

| attract | build | collect | ~~deliver~~ | measure | use |

1 These books __will be delivered__ tomorrow morning to your house.

2 The church _____ in the 15th century, but now it's a library.

3 Huge rocks _____ to build Stonehenge in England.

4 The ingredients _____ carefully, but the cake still tasted strange.

5 Old clothes _____ at the school, and we'll give them all away to charity.

6 The picnic is terrible! These flies _____ to the food. They're everywhere!

3 ⭐⭐ Complete the conversation with the correct form of the verbs in parentheses.

CHRIS Hey, Alison! Let's see if you can answer these questions.

ALISON A quiz? Sure.

CHRIS OK, first question. How many languages [1] __are spoken__ (speak) in India?

ALISON Umm … it's a lot; I know that. Two hundred?

CHRIS No, four hundred! Next one: When [2] _____ the first phone app _____ (create)?

ALISON I think it was 1998.

CHRIS Very good! What [3] _____ (measure) in megabits per second?

ALISON That's easy! Your internet connection speed.

CHRIS And … where [4] _____ 5.6 million cars _____ (produce) in 2017?

ALISON Umm … France?

CHRIS No, it was in Germany. So, after all your hard work, would you like some lunch?

ALISON Great idea. But first, answer this question. What [5] _____ (deliver) by drones in the future?

CHRIS That's obvious … pizza!

4 ⭐⭐⭐ Write five passive sentences about smartphones. Use these ideas.

1 What are they made of?

2 Where are they produced?

3 What year was an important model produced?

4 How are apps downloaded?

5 How will they be used in the future?

_____

_____

_____

_____

VOCABULARY AND LISTENING
Extreme Adjectives

1 ⭐ (Circle) the correct options.

We visited New York in January. It's a ¹*stunning* / *terrifying* city, with its long straight avenues and ²*boiling* / *marvelous* buildings. The weather in the city can be extreme: the heat in the summer can be ³*deafening* / *awful*, and there can be very low temperatures in the winter. It snowed while we were there, so Central Park was ⁴*deafening* / *gorgeous*, all covered in snow, but I had to buy a new hat and gloves because it was ⁵*freezing* / *boiling*! We took the subway to Wall Street – the noise of the trains was ⁶*deafening* / *enormous*, but it was ⁷*stunning* / *fascinating* to see so many people from all around the world living together in this ⁸*enormous* / *awful* city.

2 ⭐⭐ Complete the sentences with adjectives from Exercise 1.

1 Can I borrow your gloves? My hands are _freezing_ .

2 Turn down that music! It's _____.

3 I couldn't watch the end of that horror movie. It was

_____.

4 Ms. Griffin's a very interesting teacher, and her history classes are _____.

5 I didn't realize the London Eye was really this big! It's

_____!

6 When we were in Oaxaca in July, it was _____: 39°C!

7 Paul had a _____ vacation – he went to Sweden and Norway, and he had a great time.

8 Ana's brother is a fashion model – he's totally _____!

9 The view from the top of the mountain was absolutely

_____.

3 ⭐⭐⭐ Complete the sentences so they are true for you.

1 When it's boiling in the summer, I _____.

2 When it's freezing in the winter, I _____.

3 The most terrifying experience I've ever had was when I

_____.

4 You can get a stunning view of my town/city if you go to

_____.

5 A fascinating fact that I know is _____.

A Virtual Reality Tour

🎧 4 ⭐ Listen to a virtual tour of the Eiffel Tower. Match the numbers 1–5 with what they refer to a–e. (See the *Learn to Learn* tip in the Student's Book, p62.)

5.01

1 1889	c	a pieces
2 1887	☐	b visitors
3 300	☐	c year of the World Fair
4 18,000	☐	d height in meters
5 7 million	☐	e year building was begun

🎧 5 ⭐⭐ Listen again. Answer the questions with two to four words.

5.01

1 What is the first image in the tour?
the original drawing

2 How long after the French Revolution did they build the Eiffel Tower?

_____

3 What were the professions of the men who helped Gustave Eiffel?

_____

4 Where were the pieces of the tower produced? _____

5 When it was finished, what did the Parisians call the Eiffel Tower?

_____

6 ⭐⭐⭐ Look up some facts about the Eiffel Tower. Write three things you found out about it.

_____

_____

_____

GRAMMAR IN ACTION
Question Tags

1 ⭐ **Match the sentences 1-8 with the question tags a-h.**

1 It's freezing,	d	a do I?
2 You stayed at a hotel in London,	☐	b can you?
3 She won't waste any money,	☐	c didn't you?
		d isn't it?
4 Mark has red hair,	☐	e does it?
5 You can't solve this math problem,	☐	f doesn't he?
		g aren't you?
6 This museum doesn't attract a lot of people,	☐	h will she?
7 You are coming to dinner,	☐	
8 I don't have to clean my room,	☐	

2 ⭐⭐ **Complete the sentences with the correct question tags.**

1 We don't have to go to school tomorrow, _____do we_____?

2 Pat and Tim have tickets for us, too, _____?

3 Sofia listens to a lot of music, _____?

4 You'll send me a message when you get there, _____?

5 Laura can speak Spanish, _____?

6 Andre has never been to Chicago before, _____?

7 It's going to be cold outside, _____?

8 Alex won't make that mistake again, _____?

3 ⭐⭐ **Complete the questions with the correct words.**

1 __You're__ not scared, are you?

2 He can't be serious, _____ he?

3 The food _____ be collected later, won't it?

4 You aren't looking for her, _____ you?

5 Ian clearly doesn't like Fiona, _____ he?

6 The pictures were beautiful, _____ they?

4 ⭐⭐⭐ **Use the prompts to write questions with question tags.**

1 A Hi, Tomás.
   I / can call / you / Tom / ?
   I can call you Tom, can't I?

   B Yes, of course. Everyone calls me Tom.

2 A I'm nervous about the English exam.

   B you / study / every night / ?
   _____

3 A That's a gorgeous bag.
   it / make of / wool / ?
   _____

   B Yes, it is. It's a traditional Peruvian bag. I bought it last year.

4 A We're going out for pizza after class.
   you / will come with us / ?
   _____

   B Yes, of course. See you later.

5 ⭐⭐⭐ **Write four sentences with question tags you could use to start a conversation with a person you've just met for the first time.**

_____

_____

_____

_____

WRITING
A Competition Entry

1 **Read the competition entry. Which of these topics is not mentioned?**

a origins of the city

b population

c famous places to visit

d the food

THE BEST CITY I'VE EVER VISITED

HOME | **STORIES** | PHOTOS

London attracts millions of visitors, and on my last visit I understood why. It's a fascinating city, and it has many marvelous places to visit.

The first town was built there by the Romans around 2,000 years ago on the River Thames. The city grew and now has a population of almost nine million! London is enormous – this is the fact that impressed me most, and you are reminded of it when you fly into one of its airports.

There are a lot of places to visit in the city, but the highlight of any visit to London is the London Eye. This huge Ferris wheel was opened in 2000 and is located next to the Thames, near Westminster Bridge. It moves around very slowly, but when you finally get to the top, you are 135 meters high, and the views from there are stunning.

I'm absolutely certain that London deserves to win because it has so many incredible places to visit! Without a doubt, London is the best city in the world to visit!

---

2 **Read the entry again and answer the questions.**

1 How old is London? _____ *over 2,000 years old*

2 What most impressed the writer about the city?

_____

3 Where is the London Eye?

_____

4 How tall is it? _____

5 Why does London deserve to win the competition?

_____

_____

3 **How does the writer express these ideas? Find the *Useful Language* phrases in the text.**

1 what was most amazing

this is the fact that impressed me the most

2 the best part of a visit

_____

3 I'm sure

_____

4 it should win

_____

5 it is certain

_____

PLAN

4 **Write a competition entry. Think of the best city you have ever visited. Take notes in your notebook about these things.**

- A short introduction to the city
- General facts about the place
- A detailed description of what impressed you
- Why the place should win

WRITE

5 **Write your competition entry. Remember to include four paragraphs, the passive, extreme adjectives, and phrases from the *Useful Language* box (see Student's Book, p65.)**

CHECK

6 **Do you ...**

- give an introduction?
- describe its highlights?
- explain why you think the place should win?

5 REVIEW

VOCABULARY

1 Match the words in the box with the definitions 1–8. There are two words you don't need.

> awful   boiling   create   deafening
> enormous   freezing   gorgeous
> measure   solve   waste

1 very cold _____

2 make something new _____

3 to use too much of something
_____

4 very loud _____

5 find the answer to _____

6 find out the size of something
_____

7 very bad _____

8 very beautiful _____

2 (Circle) the correct options.

1 My phone is *connected / communicated* to Wi-Fi, but the video isn't playing.

2 Vero thought the movie was *fascinating / boiling*, but I fell asleep after 20 minutes.

3 Some of the scenes in the horror movie were *gorgeous / terrifying* – I couldn't watch.

4 What time will my new computer be *solved / delivered* tomorrow?

5 Olives are *collected / supplied* by shaking the tree really hard so that they all fall on the ground.

6 The wedding was *deafening / marvelous*, and the bride's dress was *stunning / terrifying*.

7 A lot of insects were *developed / attracted* by the smell of the food.

8 Several *enormous / freezing* rocks fell from the side of the mountain.

GRAMMAR IN ACTION

3 Complete the text with correct passive form of the verbs in parentheses.

Help Us Fix the Castle

Originally, to build the old castle, enormous rocks ¹_____ (collect) from the mountains near here, and they ²_____ (deliver) by teams of hundreds of people pulling them. The thick walls ³_____ all _____ (create) by hand, and the rocks ⁴_____ (measure) very carefully because they had to go together perfectly.

Now all the rocks are lying on the ground, so each rock ⁵_____ (pull) up and then it ⁶_____ (drop) into the right place. We're making good progress.

Next year, we will start on the roof. The roof ⁷_____ (make) of wood. Trees from the local forest ⁸_____ (cut) down, and then they ⁹_____ (bring) here.

4 Complete the sentences with question tags.

1 It's a gorgeous day, _____?

2 We can't connect the printer, _____?

3 Emily hasn't figured out the answers, _____?

4 Dennis didn't return the book, _____?

5 These problems will be solved, _____?

6 Rosanna doesn't waste any time, _____?

7 All the pieces of the table have been measured, _____?

8 Bees produce honey, _____?

5 Complete the conversation with the missing words. (Circle) the correct options.

EMILIA What [1]_____ to do for the physics presentation next week?

GEORGE I'm not sure. I [2]_____ do something about the tallest buildings in the world.

EMILIA That's ... umm ... different. I mean ... doing something about the stars and planets is easier, [3]_____?

GEORGE Well, I [4]_____ this documentary about the Jeddah Tower yesterday – it's in Saudi Arabia. When it's finished, it's going to be the tallest building they'll [5]_____.

EMILIA How tall is the one in Dubai?

GEORGE The Burj Khalifa? That's only 828 meters tall. This one will be [6]_____ bigger! They [7]_____ to make it a mile high – that's 1.6 kilometers – but there were too many problems with that. They think it'll be over one kilometer.

EMILIA Seriously? That's [8]_____ enormous. But what do you mean "they think"?

GEORGE Well, it could be [9]_____ taller than one kilometer. They're not sure yet.

EMILIA I [10]_____ believe they actually don't know. Someone [11]_____ know.

GEORGE Well, of course, but it's a secret, I think.

EMILIA So, when are they going to finish it?

GEORGE Well, [12]_____ on it since 2013, and they [13]_____ it for around eight years.

EMILIA That's amazing, isn't it?

GEORGE Yeah ... and to think the tallest thing in the world [14]_____ the Eiffel Tower.

EMILIA Anyway, so what does all this have to do with the physics presentation?

1 a do you do	b you will do	c are you going	d may you do
2 a must	b should	c must not	d might
3 a it is	b doesn't it	c isn't it	d won't it
4 a had watched	b used to watch	c watched	d have watched
5 a have never built	b ever build	c have ever built	d already have built
6 a a little	b far	c really	d fairly
7 a have planned	b had planned	c have been planning	d will have planned
8 a really	b extremely	c a lot	d a little
9 a pretty	b absolutely	c really	d a bit
10 a must not	b don't have to	c shouldn't	d can't
11 a doesn't	b must	c can't	d may
12 a they've been working	b they're working	c they work	d they'll be working
13 a 'll build	b 're going to build	c 'll be building	d build
14 a would be	b is	c used to be	d had been

6 When do you push the limits?

VOCABULARY

Verb Collocations with *To Get*, *To Take*, and *To Have*

1 ⭐ **Complete the chart with the words and phrases in the box.**

> ~~advantage of~~   a lot out of
> an interest in   bored   doubts   fun
> lost   on my nerves   pleasure in   risks
> the chance   to know

To Get	To Have	To Take
		advantage of

2 ⭐⭐ **Match the beginnings of the sentences 1–6 with the endings a–f.**

1 Oscar has really been getting ___a___
2 Sergio actually takes ⬜
3 How did you get ⬜
4 Victor really got ⬜
5 I had never taken ⬜
6 Chefs shouldn't take ⬜

a on my nerves lately.
b lost on your way to school?
c risks when they're chopping food – they might cut themselves!
d an interest in doing anything dangerous before.
e pleasure in eating really spicy food.
f a lot out of his time in San Francisco – his English is a lot better.

3 ⭐⭐ **Complete the conversation with one word in each blank.**

MIA   What's the matter?

ROSE   It's Laura again. She's really ¹ _getting_ on my nerves.

MIA   What did she do?

ROSE   Well, I'd just like her to take an interest ² _____ the things I like doing. She just says she ³ _____ bored when she's with my friends.

MIA   That's not fair. She should try getting to ⁴ _____ them. She ⁵ _____ the chance to join our group at the party on Friday, and she didn't take advantage ⁶ _____ it. She just stood in the corner on her own!

ROSE   Exactly! When we go out with her friends, I always try to ⁷ _____ fun. I'm having ⁸ _____ about our friendship!

4 ⭐⭐⭐ **Complete the sentences so they are true for you. (See the *Learn to Learn* tip in the Student's Book, p71.)**

1 When I get lost, I _____.
2 It really gets on my nerves when _____.
3 I always have fun when I _____.
4 I once had the chance to _____, but I didn't do it!

Explore It! 🖱️

Guess the correct answer.

What is the most dangerous job in the world?

a a lumberjack (a person who cuts down trees)   b a firefighter   c an astronaut

Find another interesting fact about dangerous jobs. Write a question and send it to a classmate in an email, or ask them in the next class.

READING
An Article

1 ⭐ **Read the text. Which two places have Mari and Patricio lived in?** _____

2 ⭐⭐ **Look at the words in bold in the text. Use them to complete the sentences.**

1 A long time ago, humans used to ____hunt____ for all their meat.

2 When we visited the village, we stayed in a _____.

3 I find that very hard to believe. It sounds _____.

4 In the desert, we met a _____ who lived in tents.

5 Eliza _____ that she made a mistake.

6 There are a lot of interesting animals and plants in the _____.

3 ⭐⭐ **Read the text again and (circle) the correct options.**

1 In this text, the writer is trying to …

   a encourage people to visit Ecuador.

   b give her opinion of Patricio and Mari's relationship.

   c show how difficult it is to live in England.

   (d) explain why Mari decided to go and live in Ecuador.

2 What does the writer think of Mari's actions?

   a She agrees that they are ridiculous.

   b She admires Mari because she wasn't afraid.

   c She finds it hard to believe.

   d She's amazed by the story of how Mari met Patricio.

3 Patricio went back to Ecuador because he …

   a found a job building houses.

   b wanted to spend more time with his daughter.

   c didn't like living so far from his community.

   d couldn't find work in Essex.

4 What does Mari think about her new life?

   a It isn't easy for her because everything is different.

   b She misses the life she had in Essex.

   c It's difficult because she can't catch fish.

   d She would like to go back to her family and business.

Moving to the Jungle

If you had the chance to give up everything to go and live in the Amazon jungle, would you do it? You would certainly have to be very brave, but 52-year-old Mari Muench took the risk.

Her story, which even she describes as "completely **ridiculous**," started in 2010 when she was on vacation in Ecuador. There she met Patricio, who is a shaman in his **tribe**. Patricio asked Mari to dance, and as they got to know each other, he told her an amazing story. He said that when he was just 15 years old, he had a dream in which he saw her. Mari also felt a very strong connection to the place. "Unless I come to live here with Patricio," she thought, "I'll never be happy."

A few months after this first meeting, Mari and Patricio got married! Then they decided to move to Essex, near London, where their daughter Samai was born. But Patricio had many doubts about living so far from his community.

So Patricio moved back to Ecuador and took advantage of the time there to begin making preparations for Mari and Samai's arrival. With help from his tribe, over a period of four months, he cleared a small piece of land in the **rainforest** and built a traditional **hut** using only materials from the forest, his hands, and a lot of hard work.

In 2018, Mari left her Essex home, her family, and her successful go-karting business, as well as the advantages of modern life, for the Ecuadorian jungle. After a two-day journey, Mari and Samai reached Patricio's community. Mari is learning how to **hunt** and fish, eat insects, and share her life with her new family. "It's the hardest thing I've ever done," she **admits**, but she says she's very happy.

4 ⭐⭐⭐ **What do you think life will be like for Mari, Patricio, and Samai? Write four sentences.**

_____

_____

_____

GRAMMAR IN ACTION
First and Second Conditional

1 ⭐ **Match the beginnings of the sentences 1–5 with the ends a–e.**

1 If you had the chance, [d]
2 We'll almost certainly get lost [ ]
3 Unless he pays attention, [ ]
4 Mateo would work harder [ ]
5 If you had a blog, [ ]

a he won't get a lot out of Mr. Smith's classes.
b I would read it.
c unless we stop and ask someone.
d would you fly in a helicopter?
e if you encouraged him more.

2 ⭐⭐ **Complete the second sentence so that it means the same as the first. Use no more than three words.**

1 In case of any doubts, you can call me.
If you __have__ any doubts, you can call me.

2 Without taking risks, you'd get really bored.
You'd get really bored if you _____ _____ any risks.

3 You don't like Rafael because you don't really know him.
You'd really like Rafael if you _____ _____ to know him.

4 I'll put the cat out in the yard if he annoys you.
I'll put the cat out in the yard _____ _____ on your nerves.

5 You can get a lot out of playing team sports.
_____ _____ team sports, you can get a lot of them.

3 ⭐⭐ **Complete the conversation with the correct form of the verbs in parentheses.**

GRETA What are you doing, James?

JAMES I'm making pizza. If you ¹ __'re__ (be) nice to me, I ² _____ (give) you a slice.

GRETA Great. But if you ³ _____ (put) pineapple on it, I ⁴ _____ (not eat) it.

JAMES Well, if you ⁵ _____ (not like) pineapple, I think I ⁶ _____ (put) some extra chunks on it!

GRETA Come on, James. If I ⁷ _____ (make) pizza, I ⁸ _____ (not use) any ingredients you didn't like.

JAMES That's true – but you don't cook! If you ever want to learn, I ⁹ _____ (help) you.

GRETA Oh, please. You only know how to make pizza! If I ¹⁰ _____ (take) an interest in cooking, I ¹¹ _____ (ask) Mom or Dad to help me.

JAMES OK, that's it! Extra chunks of pineapple!

4 ⭐⭐ <u>Underline</u> **and correct one mistake in each sentence.**

1 If I <u>have</u> a drone, I would fly it really fast. _____had_____

2 If you folded your clothes properly, your room won't be such a mess. _____

3 Will we get lost if we won't follow the map?
_____

4 If I listen to classical music, it might be inspire me.
_____

5 Unless you don't try it, you'll never know what it's like.
_____

6 What you would do if you had doubts about your future?
_____

5 ⭐⭐⭐ **Complete the sentences with your own ideas.**

1 If I knew how to cook well, _____ ___

2 If I had a blog, _____ .

3 I would take more risks if _____ .

4 Unless I fail all my exams, _____ .

5 If I get a really good job, _____ .

6 If I get bored later, _____ .

VOCABULARY AND LISTENING

Inspiration and Challenge

A Radio Show

1 ⭐ **Find nine more words connected with challenges in the word search.**

E	N	C	O	U	R	A	G	E	I	D	G
N	F	A	P	T	X	C	N	I	R	E	D
I	N	S	P	I	R	E	T	A	S	T	C
B	E	R	O	B	S	T	A	C	L	E	H
X	O	B	R	A	V	E	R	Y	B	R	A
Q	V	T	T	O	R	Z	T	T	O	M	L
P	E	F	U	U	T	Y	B	G	O	I	L
U	R	C	N	R	G	U	D	V	Y	N	E
A	C	H	I	E	V	E	W	O	R	A	N
L	O	T	T	P	V	I	S	A	E	T	G
V	M	W	I	P	L	D	A	Q	W	I	E
B	E	X	E	R	W	A	U	X	D	O	K
R	U	S	S	U	P	P	O	R	T	N	E

2 ⭐⭐ **Match the words from Exercise 1 with the definitions.**

1 You'll need this in a dangerous situation.
   _____bravery_____

2 My parents do this so that I read more books.
   _____

3 You'll have to go around or over it.
   _____

4 Your family and friends will always do this.
   _____

5 An extraordinary person does this to other people.
   _____

6 You'll need to work hard when you have one.
   _____

7 When you keep trying and never give up, you have this. _____

8 You do this if you deal with something successfully.
   _____

9 If you're lucky, you have these. _____

10 When you reach your goal, you do this.
   _____

3 ⭐⭐⭐ **Write a paragraph about someone who acted with bravery. You can write a true story or invent one.**

_____

_____

_____

_____

🎧 **4** 6.01 ⭐ **Listen to the radio show about what people think is "risky behavior." Put the pictures in the order you hear about them.**

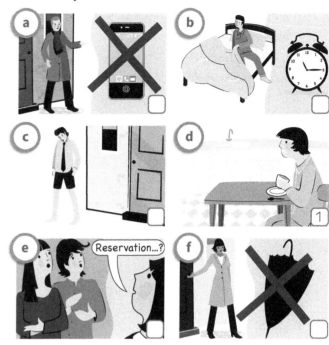

🎧 **5** 6.01 ⭐⭐ **Listen again and circle the correct options. (See the *Learn to Learn* tip in the Student's Book, p74.)**

1 How many people took part in the survey?
   a 2,000   **b** over 2,000   **c** 40

2 People think it's risky to drink coffee or tea before ....
   a going out   **b** having breakfast   **c** going to bed

3 What do people think is risky when they go to a restaurant?
   a ordering foreign food
   b going without making a reservation
   c reserving a table after 11 p.m.

4 What shouldn't you do with your smartphone?
   a leave it charging for too long
   b take it everywhere you go
   c leave it at home

5 People also think it's risky to leave the house ....
   a with different shoes or socks
   b with wet hair
   c in their pajamas

GRAMMAR IN ACTION
Third Conditional

1 ⭐ **Match the sentences 1–4 with the pictures a–d.**

1 If Charlie had missed the bus, he wouldn't have met Hannah. `d`

2 If Charlie hadn't missed the bus, he wouldn't have arrived late. ☐

3 If I hadn't gone to the party, I wouldn't have had so much fun. ☐

4 I would have gone to the party if I hadn't agreed to watch a movie with Suzy. ☐

a

b

c

d

2 ⭐⭐ **Complete the sentences with the correct form of the verbs in parentheses.**

TO: Aisha

FROM: Amy

Hi Aisha,

I'm never going to have a party in my house again! First of all, if I ¹ ___hadn't invited___ (not invite) so many people, there ² _____ (be) more food for everyone. Then, Caro and Elsa ³ _____ (not get) lost if I ⁴ _____ (send) them a map. I don't think inviting Tomás was a good idea, either. If he ⁵ _____ (not jump) on the sofa, he ⁶ _____ (not break) the mirror in the living room.

There was one good thing. If Mira ⁷ _____ (not come), she ⁸ _____ (not bring) her friend Beatriz. She's from Brazil, and she invited me to stay with her when I go traveling this summer!

Amy

3 ⭐⭐⭐ **Complete the second sentence so that it means the same as the first. Use no more than three words.**

1 Holly didn't have the same opportunities as everyone else, so she didn't go to college.

If Holly ___had had___ the same opportunities as everyone else, she would have gone to college.

2 George didn't take any interest, so he failed the exam.

If George had taken an interest, he _____ failed the exam.

3 The fish didn't taste very good because of the sauce.

The fish _____ better if it hadn't had that sauce.

4 My friend Mike went to the hospital last week because he broke his leg playing soccer.

Mike wouldn't have gone to the hospital if he _____ his leg playing soccer.

5 The party turned out really well because the music was amazing.

The party wouldn't _____ out so well if the music hadn't been so amazing.

4 ⭐⭐⭐ **Answer the questions with your own ideas.**

1 What would you have done if you hadn't come to school today?

_____

2 If you'd been born 50 years ago, what would your childhood have been like?

_____

WRITING
A For and Against Essay

1 ⭐ **Read the essay. Is the writer in favor of or against taking risks?** _____

A Life Without Risks Is Boring

1 It's difficult to imagine a life without risk. ¹_____ For example, we take risks every day when we leave the house. In fact, doctors say your home is the most dangerous place in the world!

2 ²_____ the one hand, some people take pleasure in dangerous situations. For ³_____, they think that if they don't do something dangerous, ⁴_____ as climbing mountains, they'll get bored. Some people argue that they are overcoming obstacles with determination.

3 On the ⁵_____ hand, many people would rather live a quiet life. They don't need to challenge themselves every day. ⁶_____, they say that you can get a lot out of life by having fun without taking risks.

4 ⁷_____ conclusion, it seems to me that if you live your life worrying about the dangers around you, you'll never be happy. However, I personally ⁸_____ you shouldn't take too many risks. You only live once, they say. That could mean take risks because you only have one life, but it can also mean that you should stay alive if you can.

2 ⭐⭐ **Complete the *Useful Language* phrases in the essay with the words in the box.**

> believe ~~for~~ furthermore in instance on other such

3 ⭐⭐ **Read the essay again. Complete the sentences.**

1 Doctors say our homes are _____.
2 Some people get bored if they don't _____.
3 Many people would prefer _____.
4 "You only live once" can mean _____ or _____.

4 **Read the essay again. Which paragraph (1–4) …**

a explains the reasons against the argument? ___

b summarizes the writer's general opinion? ___

c introduces the argument ___

d explains the reasons for the argument? ___

PLAN

5 ⭐⭐ **Look at the essay title and take notes on your arguments in favor of and against the statement.**

> Life Is Just About Having Fun

In favor: _____
_____
_____
_____

Against: _____
_____
_____

6 ⭐⭐ **Decide what information to include in each paragraph. Use the information from Exercise 4 to help you.**

WRITE

7 ⭐⭐⭐ **Write your essay. Remember to include four paragraphs, conditional sentences, vocabulary from this unit, and phrases from the *Useful Language* box (see Student's Book, p77).**

CHECK

8 **Do you …**
- include an introduction?
- talk about negatives?
- talk about positives?
- have a conclusion?

VOCABULARY

1 Complete the expressions with *get*, *have*, or *take*.

1 _____ on my nerves
2 _____ advantage of
3 _____ fun
4 _____ risks
5 _____ bored
6 _____ doubts
7 _____ an interest in
8 _____ a lot out of
9 _____ pleasure in
10 _____ to know
11 _____ lost
12 _____ the chance

2 Complete the sentences with the words in the box.

> achieve   bravery   challenge   determination
> encouraged   inspired   obstacles
> opportunities   overcome   support

1 We went to the stadium on Saturday to _____ our soccer team.
2 When Paola moved to Moscow, the biggest _____ was learning to speak Russian.
3 If you fail this test, they won't give you any more _____ .
4 My parents _____ me to learn how to play the piano, and now I'm a professional musician.
5 Rescuing that dog from the river took a lot of _____ .
6 We were losing 3–0, but our _____ helped us to come back and win 4–3.
7 Liz was _____ to write this song by things that happened when she was young.
8 Everyone has to _____ many _____ throughout their lives – that's life.
9 Gonzalo had to work very hard to _____ his dream of becoming a dancer.

GRAMMAR IN ACTION

3 Put the words in the correct order to make first and second conditional sentences.

1 I / the teacher / the answer / I'd ask / If / didn't know / .

_____

2 have to / If / you / Peter / have / ask / you'll / any / doubts / .

_____

3 message / send / you / If / I / bored / get / I'll / a / .

_____

4 you / dreams / you'll / Unless / achieve / your / never / try harder / .

_____

5 risky / I / do / it / wouldn't / was / I / thought / it / If / .

_____

6 anything / this obstacle / You'll / you / never / overcome / unless / achieve / .

_____

4 Complete the third conditional sentences with the correct form of the verbs in parentheses.

1 If I _____ (get) lost, I _____ (not arrive) on time.
2 He _____ (do) better in the race if you _____ (encourage) him more.
3 Steve _____ (not say) anything if you _____ (not get) on his nerves.
4 I _____ (not be) able to buy a new phone if I _____ (not save) all my allowance for months!
5 If you _____ (not sit) in the back, you _____ (hear) everything the teacher said.

5 Complete the interview with the missing words. (Circle) the correct options.

INTERVIEWER So why did you decide to become a soccer player?

JULIA I suppose it's like everyone. I ¹_____ love playing when I was a child. I always had fun playing soccer. But if I ²_____ the support of my family, I would never ³_____ a professional.

INTERVIEWER ⁴_____ hard for you?

JULIA Yes, sometimes. When I was younger, I had doubts about my ability. But then my coach ⁵_____ an interest in me, and I ⁶_____ to improve and to get ⁷_____ better than I was. I knew I ⁸_____ improve my skills if I wanted to achieve my dreams.

INTERVIEWER You don't get bored with soccer, ⁹_____?

JULIA No, I don't. ¹⁰_____ pleasure in training, and my teammates really inspire me. I wouldn't be happy ¹¹_____ I wasn't training and playing soccer, and there are thousands of people there to support me every week. How ¹²_____ I get bored?

1 a would	b used to	c could	d had to
2 a hadn't had	b hadn't	c haven't had	d haven't
3 a become	b became	c have become	d to become
4 a Is it	b Was it	c Has it been	d Had it been
5 a take	b took	c had taken	d might take
6 a was encouraged	b encouraged	c am encouraged	d encourages
7 a bit	b fairly	c totally	d far
8 a must	b will have to	c would have needed	d would have to
9 a do you	b don't you	c are you	d were you
10 a I'm always taking	b I was always taking	c I've always taken	d I could always take
11 a if	b unless	c when	d after
12 a must	b could	c should	d may

7 Why are emotions important?

VOCABULARY
Feelings

1 ⭐ **Complete the adjectives with the correct vowels. Then complete the chart with the adjectives.**

1 r i d i c u l o u s
2 gr _ t _ f _ l
3 h _ rt
4 d _ wn
5 gl _ d
6 p _ _ c _ f _ l
7 _ ns _ c _ r _

8 _ m _ s _ d
9 _ _ g _ r
10 _ nn _ y _ d
11 h _ p _ f _ l
12 thr _ ll _ d
13 s _ t _ sf _ _ d

Positive 🙂	Negative ☹

2 ⭐⭐ (Circle) **the correct options.**

1 Please don't post that photo. I look *peaceful* / *ridiculous*!

2 What did you do? Why is Emily so *annoyed* / *grateful* with you?

3 Marcos needs your help. He's feeling *glad* / *insecure* about his class project.

4 If they knew it was raining, they wouldn't be so *amused* / *eager* to go out.

5 My math teacher isn't *satisfied* / *hopeful* with my work. She thinks I can do better.

6 Kathy's *thrilled* / *down* because she's getting a new phone.

3 ⭐⭐ **Complete the sentences with correct adjectives from Exercise 1.**

1 Lucas is ____hurt____ because you didn't invite him to the party. You should say you're sorry.

2 I'm so _____ you called because I wanted to ask you something.

3 I like studying in the backyard because it's so _____ – all you can hear are the birds singing.

4 Liam's feeling _____ because his best friend has just moved to Germany.

5 The teacher wasn't very _____ with my joke, so she gave me extra homework.

6 We're taking a big risk, but we're all _____ that everything will turn out well.

4 ⭐⭐⭐ **Write a sentence describing how you would feel if these things happened to you. Explain why. (See the *Learn to Learn* tip in the Student's Book, p83.)**

How would you feel if …

1 you had to make dinner for your family?

_____

2 one of your relatives gave you some money?

_____

3 a friend of yours told you she was moving to another city?

_____

4 your teacher told you that you had an exam tomorrow?

_____

5 you remembered it was a holiday while waiting for the school bus?

_____

Explore It!

Guess the correct answers (choose two options).

Dogs can recognize whether a human is angry or happy by … .

a their facial expression   c the tone of their voice

b the words they use

Find another interesting fact about an animal that can recognize human emotions. Write a question and send it to a classmate in an email, or ask them in the next class.

READING
A Magazine Interview

1 ⭐ **Read the interview. Is this sentence true or false?**

Mindfulness doesn't help students with their exams.

2 ⭐⭐ **Look at the <u>underlined</u> words in the interview. Use them to complete the sentences.**

1 I can't _concentrate_ if you keep talking. You're getting on my nerves.
2 Humans have five _____: hearing, sight, taste, smell, and touch.
3 Santiago improved his _____ in tennis with practice.
4 Dr. Morgan has done many _____ about stress.
5 That car has a very _____ engine. It's the fastest car in the world.
6 The doctor told my dad that if he _____ his weight, he'll be healthier.

3 ⭐⭐ **Read the interview again and (circle) the correct options.**

1 Jeremy Parker says that *concentration* / (*mindfulness*) can stop people from having negative feelings.
2 Mindfulness teaches us to pay more attention to *the present* / *difficult situations*.
3 Meditation is used to *control our feelings* / *make us happy*.
4 When we're depressed, *we sometimes make ourselves* / *other people sometimes make us* feel even worse.
5 Cognitive therapy *studies how mindfulness works* / *can teach people to understand their feelings*.
6 Safari Walk is *not difficult to learn* / *especially good for children*.

4 ⭐⭐⭐ **Answer the questions so they are true for you.**

1 What do you do when you feel down or insecure?

_____

2 Would you like to learn more about mindfulness? Why / Why not?

_____

Mindfulness for Students

Sometimes you're worried and insecure about everything, and you can't <u>concentrate</u>. These feelings affect your personal life and your schoolwork and can sometimes get worse. The psychologist Jeremy Parker (and many other experts) suggests using mindfulness.

What is mindfulness?

Mindfulness is a very <u>powerful</u> tool or <u>technique</u> that helps people concentrate more on the here and now. It helps you stay calm in difficult situations, which you often create for yourself. The technique teaches you to practice breathing and uses meditation to calm you down and understand your feelings and thoughts.

How does mindfulness help?

Everyone has times when they feel down or they feel hurt for some reason. Your mind is full of negative feelings, and there's a voice inside you telling you that you're a failure or that you're useless. Through meditation, you learn not to listen to that voice and after a time ... the voice stops. So you stop worrying about things so much, and you avoid thinking those negative thoughts.

What is the science behind mindfulness?

There's an area of psychology called "cognitive therapy" that helps people understand how they are thinking and change it. Mindfulness is based on this, and many <u>studies</u> show that it works. One study, for example, showed that meditating before an exam helps you get better grades. Another study shows that it <u>reduces</u> stress and worry.

Can you give an example of a mindfulness activity?

There's a simple activity called "Safari Walk." It works for children, adolescents, and adults, and it's very simple: you walk somewhere, and while you're walking, you notice everything. You listen to the sounds of birds singing, you look at the colors of things – you use all your <u>senses</u> to be in the moment. And you feel peaceful and happy.

GRAMMAR IN ACTION
Gerunds and Infinitives (with *to*)

1 ⭐ Circle the correct options.

1 *Getting* / *To get* lost on the way to school is not normal.

2 It's important *taking* / *to take* advantage of the opportunities you are given.

3 George says he enjoys *cooking* / *to cook*, but he doesn't have time.

4 I tasted the sauce *checking* / *to check* if it was too spicy.

5 She decided not *to wear* / *wearing* her new boots to the party.

6 I'm annoyed about *to lose* / *losing* the game.

2 ⭐⭐ Complete the conversation with the correct form of the verbs in parentheses.

MAE ¹___Going___ (go) to that mindfulness class was a great idea.

ISA Yes, it was. I'm eager ² _____ (try) it. I'd like ³ _____ (learn) a few more of Dr. Fraser's techniques.

MAE Well, first he told us to practice ⁴ _____ (breathe) … like this.

ISA Don't forget ⁵ _____ (hold) it for a few seconds.

MAE I feel a bit ridiculous, but after ⁶ _____ (do) it a few times, I know I'll feel better.

ISA ⁷ _____ (learn) something new is always a little strange at the beginning.

MAE I suppose it is. He suggested ⁸ _____ (try) it at home on our own before the next meeting.

ISA OK, I'm going home ⁹ _____ (practice). I'll send a message later ¹⁰ _____ (tell) you how it's going.

3 ⭐⭐ Complete the sentences with the correct form of the verbs in the box.

| bring   hear   look   ~~take~~   win   write |

1 After an hour of studying, I stopped ___to take___ a short break.

2 I'll never forget _____ the championship last year – I was so thrilled.

3 I remember _____ a strange noise, and then all the lights went out.

4 John didn't do his homework because he forgot _____ it down yesterday.

5 Rania stopped _____ at her phone to listen to the news.

6 Did you remember _____ a sandwich to school today? We have an extra class.

4 ⭐⭐ Match the sentences with the correct meanings.

1 I stopped to talk to Matt.

2 I stopped talking to Matt.

3 I forgot to call Lisa.

4 I forgot I called Lisa.

a I stopped what I was doing to talk to Matt.

b I don't talk to Matt anymore.

c I don't remember calling Lisa.

d I didn't call Lisa.

5 ⭐⭐⭐ Answer the questions so they are true for you. Write full sentences.

1 Do you enjoy swimming in the ocean in the summer? Why / Why not?

_____

2 What did you forget to do last week?

_____

3 Which sport would you be interested in learning to play?

_____

4 What do you hope to do when you finish school?

_____

5 What things have you stopped doing since you were a child?

_____

VOCABULARY AND LISTENING
Expressions with *Heart* and *Mind*

1 ⭐ **What word goes on the back of these flashcards? Write *heart* or *mind*. (See the *Learn to Learn* tip in the Student's Book, p86.)**

1
put his _____ into it

heart

2
learn something by _____

3
have something on your _____

4
break someone's _____

5
it crossed my _____

2 ⭐⭐ **Complete the text with one word in each blank.**

Making decisions is the hardest thing in the world. I just can't ¹ _____make_____ up my mind whether I want this or that. And then, when I've made a choice, I often have doubts. I'll have the decision ² _____ my mind for days. Suddenly, it ³ _____ my mind that the other choice might be better, and I think maybe I should ⁴ _____ my mind. And when it's something that involves other people, I have to ⁵ _____ in mind what other people think. Maybe you should choose for me!

3 ⭐⭐⭐ **Answer the questions.**

1 What was the last thing you had to learn by heart?

_____

2 What do you do when you can't make up your mind about something?

_____

3 Who do you talk to when you have something on your mind?

_____

A Conversation

🎧 7.01 **4** ⭐ **Listen to the conversation between Jack, Amy, and Valerie. What does Jack decide to do?**

_____

🎧 7.01 **5** ⭐⭐ **Listen again and answer the questions.**

1 What will Jack have to do soon?
   He'll have to take exams.

2 What does Valerie do after school?

_____

3 Why does she do it?

_____

4 What does Amy do?

_____

5 How did she feel at the beginning?

_____

6 Why don't Valerie and Amy support Jack's decision?

_____

6 ⭐⭐⭐ **Write about something you do after school. What do you do? Why did you decide to do it? What do you like about it?**

_____

_____

_____

GRAMMAR IN ACTION
Subject and Object Questions

1 ⭐ **Complete the subject questions with *Who* or *What*.**

1 A ___Who___ decided to buy this ridiculous present for Alejandro?

B It was Flavia.

2 A _____ changed your mind about the T-shirt?

B The price.

3 A _____ made such a deafening noise?

B It was thunder.

4 A _____ wants to learn all those names by heart?

B Nobody.

5 A _____ enjoyed the concert the most?

B Emilio did.

2 ⭐⭐ **Put the words in the correct order to make questions.**

1 you / exams / do / about / feeling / How / avoid / nervous / ?

How do you avoid feeling nervous about exams?

2 the / crossed / when / mind / your / drone / you / What / saw / ?

_____

3 decide / to / shopping / did / with / you / go / Who / ?

_____

4 get / is / soccer / to / game / going / at / Who / bored / a / ?

_____

5 you / annoyed / about / did / get / What / so / ?

_____

3 ⭐ **Match the answers a–e with the questions from Exercise 2.**

a My sister. She hates going to the stadium. ◯

b I thought it was a bird! ◯

c The computer – it stopped working! ◯

d Leandro came with me. I bought these jeans. ◯

e Mindfulness helps me avoid feeling nervous. ①

4 ⭐⭐⭐ **Complete the interview. Write questions with *Who* or *What* and the words given.**

A discover / your amazing ability?

[1]*Who discovered your amazing ability?*

B My coach, Alison. She saw me playing one day and told me she'd like to be my coach.

A You used to play soccer, but now you play tennis. make / you / change / your mind / ?

[2] _____

B I enjoyed them both, but I had to make up my mind, and I just loved playing tennis.

A It hasn't been easy for you. support / you in the difficult times / ? [3] _____

_____

B My family – they're amazing.

A inspire / you / ? [4] _____

B I really admire Rafael Nadal.

A Now you're number one in your country. it / feel / like / ? [5] _____

B It's amazing. I'm thrilled.

A You always seem very calm. get / on / nerves / ?

[6] _____

B A lot of things, actually. I don't like doing interviews!

5 ⭐⭐⭐ **Answer the questions so they are true for you. Write full sentences.**

1 What do you often get annoyed about?

_____

2 Who calls or sends you messages every day?

_____

3 Among your friends, who plays a musical instrument?

_____

4 Who made dinner at home last night?

_____

WRITING
An Email Reply

1 ⭐ **Read the emails. Which piece of advice does Daniel <u>not</u> give?**

1 Find a good teacher. ☐   3 Borrow a guitar. ☐

2 Buy an expensive guitar. ☐   4 Watch videos. ☐

● ● ●

TO: Daniel

FROM: Monica

Hi Daniel,

Josue told me that you took up the guitar this year. I'm hoping to learn how to play, too, but I'm not sure. Is it very difficult? Any advice?

All the best,

Monica

● ● ●

TO: Monica

FROM: Daniel

Hi Monica,

I'm so glad you wrote to me. Playing the guitar is fun, so ¹ <u>I would recommend</u> learning it. It's difficult at the beginning, so ² _____ find a teacher. My teacher was really patient, and he never got annoyed with me when I did something silly.

Also, ³ _____ to borrow someone else's guitar for the first few weeks until you're sure you enjoy it. ⁴ _____ , don't go out and buy an expensive guitar and then change your mind. Who wants to waste money like that?

You're probably eager to start learning songs, but first try to learn basic things like where to put your fingers. When you find a teacher, ⁵ _____ taking classes more often at the beginning? I took three classes a week to get a good start.

Online videos were really helpful, and I'm grateful to my teacher for suggesting that I watch them.

Anyway, good luck!

All the best,

Daniel

---

2 ⭐⭐ **Complete the email with the *Useful Language*.**

a Whatever you do

b it would definitely help to

c why don't you suggest

d ~~I would recommend~~

e it might be better

PLAN

3 ⭐⭐ **Write an email reply. Look at Laurie's email and think of pieces of advice.**

● ● ●

Hi,

I'm really insecure about my exam, and I'm feeling very nervous. Do you have any advice?

Laurie

Take notes on what you think she should and shouldn't do.

Do: _____

Don't: _____

_____

WRITE

4 ⭐⭐⭐ **Write your email reply. Remember to include your advice from Exercise 3, *Useful Language* phrases for recommending and suggesting (see Student's Book, p89), and reasons for your suggestions.**

CHECK

5 Do you ...
- say what Laurie should do?
- say what Laurie should not do?
- think the advice is useful?

7 REVIEW

VOCABULARY

1 Find 12 more feelings adjectives in the word search.

```
R  B (E  A  G  E  R) F  O  L  P  S
I  V  S  N  L  C  V  U  H  U  R  T
D  G  A  N  A  Y  A  I  N  H  V  H
I  R  T  O  D  O  W  N  N  O  P  R
C  A  I  Y  F  R  B  S  J  P  K  I
U  T  S  E  D  T  V  E  U  E  Q  L
L  E  F  D  P  E  A  C  E  F  U  L
O  F  I  A  F  Y  E  U  W  U  K  E
U  U  E  S  C  H  F  R  R  L  J  D
S  L  D  A  M  U  S  E  D  F  U  P
```

2 Complete the expressions.

1 b_____ my heart
2 c_____ my mind
3 s_____ my mind
4 c_____ to my heart
5 m_____ up my mind
6 l_____ by heart
7 p_____ my heart i_____ it
8 h_____ something on my mind
9 b_____ in mind
10 c_____ my mind

GRAMMAR IN ACTION

3 Circle the correct options: gerund (*G*) or infinitive (*I*).

1 after verbs like *decide*, *refuse*, *hope*   G   I
2 after prepositions   G   I
3 to explain purpose   G   I
4 after verbs like *avoid*, *enjoy*, *suggest*   G   I
5 as the subject of a sentence   G   I
6 after adjectives   G   I

4 Complete the sentences with the correct form of the verbs in the box.

| feel   go   help   learn   see   waste |

1 I enjoy _____ things by heart sometimes.
2 Edward is eager _____ with the preparations for the party.
3 Mindfulness can help you avoid _____ nervous.
4 I don't remember _____ to the hospital after the accident.
5 _____ time is very easy when you have a phone in your hand.
6 I connected these two cords _____ what would happen.

5 Complete the questions for the interview.

INTERVIEWER   ¹When / you / start playing basketball / ?

_____

MATT   When I was about seven years old.
INTERVIEWER   ²Who / teach / you how to play / ?

_____

MATT   My dad. He loves basketball.
INTERVIEWER   ³Who / give / you your first basketball / ?

_____

MATT   My coach, actually. Until then, I'd always played with my dad's ball.
INTERVIEWER   ⁴Who / be / your favorite player / ?

_____

MATT   LeBron James, of course.
INTERVIEWER   ⁵What / make / you feel insecure / ?

_____

MATT   Doing interviews. I never know what to say.
INTERVIEWER   ⁶Where / you / practice / ?

_____

MATT   At school. We have a very good gym.

6 Complete the text with the missing words. (Circle) the correct options.

Birds Come to Town

A small community called Broken Hill in New South Wales, Australia, has a problem. A group of emus – large Australian birds that can't fly – have decided ¹_____ in the town. It ²_____ in the region for many months, and vets believe the birds ³_____ be looking for food and water. ⁴_____ along the main street of the town is ⁵_____ strange. You can see the emus stopping to eat in yards. The vets in the area believe the birds ⁶_____ food and water by local people, and now, of course, the emus aren't very eager to leave town. Bruce Wilson, a police officer in Broken Hill, says, "If it ⁷_____, they wouldn't have come. But if people didn't give them food, they ⁸_____. This isn't a natural place for them." Local people are afraid some of the birds ⁹_____ by dogs. "What ¹⁰_____ if an emu is killed by a car?" asked another neighbor.

1 a living	b live	c lives	d to live
2 a doesn't rain	b hasn't rained	c hasn't been raining	d isn't raining
3 a might	b can	c should	d had to
4 a To walk	b Walk	c Walking	d Walks
5 a too	b a lot	c extremely	d absolutely
6 a have been giving	b have been given	c have given	d are giving
7 a rained	b has rained	c will rain	d had rained
8 a wouldn't stay	b won't stay	c don't stay	d hadn't stayed
9 a are attacked	b will be attacked	c might attack	d attacked
10 a will happen	b had happened	c happened	d does happen

8 What influences you?

VOCABULARY
Advertising

1 ⭐ Complete the crossword. Use the clues.

Across →

3 the name of a type of product
6 tell people about your product (on TV or online)
9 a person who is selling something
10 you write this to give your opinion about a product
11 a symbol that represents the product

Down ↓

1 change how someone thinks about something
2 a program that stops ads on your computer
4 the object or service a company sells
5 this type of company makes ads
7 a word or short phrase linked to a brand
8 a person who buys something

2 ⭐⭐ Complete the sentences with the correct form of the verbs in the box.

> advertise   block   ~~buy~~   market
> not influence   produce   review   sell

1 I don't want _____to buy_____ a new phone.
  This one's perfectly good.
2 A lot of the people who _____
  the book online said they didn't like it.
3 I saw those drones _____
  on TV – they look amazing.
4 Some products are very difficult
  _____ in other countries because
  of their names.
5 Do you know anyone who _____
  a bike? I need a new one.
6 Most technological devices like phones and
  tablets _____ in Asian countries.
7 A lot of people say that advertising
  _____ them – but actually it does.
8 There are so many ads on the Internet that
  sometimes I'd really like _____
  them all.

3 ⭐⭐ Look at the verbs in Exercise 2 again. What
is their noun form? (See the *Learn to Learn* tip in
the Student's Book, p95.)

1 _____buyer_____	5 _____
2 _____	6 _____
3 _____	7 _____
4 _____	8 _____

Explore It!

Guess the correct answer.

It's not true that we don't
like watching ads. An ad for
Samsung in India has had over ____ million views.

a 100   b 150   c 200

**Find another interesting fact about an ad.
Write a question and sent it to a classmate in
an email, or ask them in the next class.**

READING

A Report

1 ⭐ Read the report. In what ways can companies find out about our habits?

_____

2 ⭐⭐ Match the <u>underlined</u> words in the report with the definitions.

1 open a webpage ____*access*____

2 looking through _____

3 collect _____

4 give someone the most recent information

_____

5 information, especially facts and numbers

_____

6 suppling something for free _____

3 ⭐⭐ Are the sentences _T_ (true) or _F_ (false)? Correct the false sentences.

1 We only provide marketing companies with information when we want to.

   F. We also provide them with information without realizing it.

2 GPS is used with social media to record where we are.

_____

3 A lot of data is gathered to give users recommendations.

_____

4 Data could help public transportation users in the future.

_____

5 We don't generate much more data than we did over 20 years ago.

_____

6 Most of the figures in the last section show our internet activity in one minute.

_____

4 ⭐⭐⭐ Answer the questions in your own words.

1 Do you think companies always use our data to provide us with better services and products?

_____

2 Do you think companies know too much about us?

_____

HOW DO COMPANIES COLLECT DATA?

As Internet and social media users, we give out a lot of personal information about ourselves, which we often _want_ to provide. But there's a lot of information that we don't even realize we're <u>giving away</u>, and that marketing companies <u>gather</u> in different ways. When we click on an ad, companies know. They also know about things that we type into a search engine the people who we follow, and whose photos we are looking at on social media. Through GPS, the companies also know where we are all the time. Every time you <u>access</u> your social media, your location is registered.

How Do Companies Use Our Data?

Every time you watch a video on YouTube, that information is used to recommend another video that you might like. The same thing happens with the songs that we listen to on Spotify and the products that we buy online. Companies use <u>data</u> to match buyers to products through advertising. But it's not just about selling things: in cities, data can <u>update</u> us when the next bus or train is coming, or where there's a traffic jam. Nowadays, a lot of people use technology to provide information about their health, which they can use to make important decisions about diet or visits to the doctor.

How Much Data Do We Generate?

Three billion people use the Internet, and we produce 50,000 GB of data every second! In 1992, that figure was 100 GB of data every day. We spend almost $900,000 on Amazon and download 375,000 apps.

In one minute, people …

- watch 4.3 million videos on YouTube.
- send 187 million emails.
- send 38 million messages on WhatsApp.
- post 481,000 Tweets.

In one minute, there are …

- 3.7 million searches on Google.
- 174,000 people <u>browsing</u> photos and videos on Instagram.

HR MIN SEC 00:01:00

50,000 GB

38 m messages — 174,000 Instagram — $900,000 Amazon — 4.3 m videos — HR MIN SEC 00:01:00 — 481,000 Tweets — 187 m emails — 3.7 m searches — 375,000 apps

GRAMMAR IN ACTION

Defining Relative Clauses

1 ⭐ (Circle) the correct options.

1 The band (*that*) / *what* I listen to the most is Green Day.

2 The logo *that* / *who* the company designed looked like a bird.

3 Tom and George became friends in a school *where* / *when* they are both learning Spanish.

4 They work for a company *whose* / *who* products are sold all around the world.

5 A lot of people buy products *when* / *that* they see the ad.

2 ⭐⭐ **Complete the text with the correct relative pronouns.**

Ad-blockers are software programs ¹ ___that___ stop ads from appearing on your screen. Many people ² _____ use the Internet get annoyed with ads ³ _____ pop up on the screen, but I don't mind them. I like seeing ads from companies ⁴ _____ products I like. The Internet is a place ⁵ _____ marketing companies try to promote their brands. I don't remember a time ⁶ _____ there were no ads on the Internet. Do you?

Non-Defining Relative Clauses

3 ⭐⭐ **Complete sentences 1–5 with the correct non-defining relative clauses a–e.**

1 Sophie, ___c___, is going to college next year.

2 These products, _____, are sold on beaches in the summer.

3 Freddie used to live at 30 Wilson Road, _____.

4 Our local soccer team, _____, has just won the championship.

5 The advertising campaign, _____, will display the new logo.

a whose shirts are sponsored by my dad's company

b where a famous TV star lives now

c who lives next door to us

d which come all the way from China

e which will run from September to December

4 ⭐⭐ **Rewrite the sentences using non-defining relative clauses.**

1 This is a very popular product. This product is sold in around 50 different countries.

   This product, which is sold in 50 different countries, is very popular.

2 This ad is very funny. I've seen it about five times.

   _____

   _____

3 Mr. Cooper is very satisfied with our work. This means we'll pass the course.

   _____

   _____

4 That girl over there speaks French very well. Her sister lives in Paris.

   _____

   _____

5 Mexico has a lot of interesting places to visit. I'm going there on vacation.

   _____

   _____

6 The book is still popular. It was written 50 years ago.

   _____

   _____

VOCABULARY AND LISTENING An Interview

Internet Verbs

1 ⭐ Circle the correct prepositions.

1 Over six million people have subscribed *on* / *to* the Lego channel on YouTube.

2 If I like someone's post, I always comment *on* / *to* it and say something nice.

3 Jenna Marbles vlogs *about* / *of* makeup, her dogs, and her daily life. She has over 18 million followers.

4 Influencers say you have to work very hard to build *on* / *up* a large number of followers.

5 I tried Instagram for a while, but I take terrible photos, so I shut *up* / *down* my account.

6 The app sends you messages about new games, but you can switch *on* / *off* this option if you don't want to see them.

2 ⭐⭐ Complete the email with the correct form of the verbs in the box.

> build up   comment on   delete   follow   post
> shut down   ~~subscribe~~   switch on   vlog about

• • •

Dear subscriber,

Thank you for ¹ ___subscribing___ to our YouTube channel. You can also ² _____ us on Twitter and Instagram. Over two years, we have ³ _____ over one million followers thanks to people like you.

On this channel, we will be ⁴ _____ our favorite video games. If you would like to ⁵ _____ the videos, we'd love to hear from you, and we'd love you to ⁶ _____ ideas for new vlogs. If you follow us on Twitter, you can ⁷ _____ the option to receive new messages from us on your screen. Remember, rude posts will be ⁸ _____ . If you continue to make rude comments, your account will be reported, and it might be ⁹ _____ .

3 ⭐ Guess which numbers in the box match the sentences.

> 300   50 million   5 billion
> over 1 billion   ~~2005~~

1 This is the year YouTube started.
   ___2005___

2 This is the number of YouTube users. _____

3 This is the number of people making videos. _____

4 This is the number of hours of video posted to YouTube every minute. _____

5 This is the number of videos watched every day. _____

🎧 8.01 **4** ⭐⭐ Listen to an interview about the YouTube video channel. Check your answers to Exercise 3.

🎧 8.01 **5** ⭐⭐ Listen again. Are the sentences *T* (true) or *F* (false)? Correct the false sentences

1 Three young men started YouTube after an argument at a dinner party.

   F. They decided they wanted to share videos from a dinner party but found it difficult.

2 Janelle believes that young people watch YouTube more than TV.

   _____

   _____

3 Product review videos are not that popular.

   _____

   _____

4 People watch YouTube to find out how to do things or how good things are.

   _____

   _____

5 One of the most popular YouTubers makes documentaries.

   _____

   _____

GRAMMAR IN ACTION
Indefinite, Reflexive, and Reciprocal Pronouns

1 ⭐ (Circle) the correct indefinite pronouns.

1 (Someone) / *Anyone* posted this video about my neighborhood.

2 I don't know *nobody* / *anybody* who vlogs about video games.

3 I swear I didn't delete *anything* / *something* from your computer.

4 What's that noise? Is *anybody* / *nobody* there?

5 He's joined Instagram, but *anyone* / *no one* follows him yet.

6 I switched on the computer, but *anything* / *nothing* happened.

2 ⭐⭐ Complete the text with the words in the box.

> anything   ~~nobody~~   nothing (x2)
> someone (x2)   something (x2)

Be careful with what you post on social media because ¹ ___nobody___ likes rude comments. My grandma used to say, "If you have ² _____ nice to say, don't say ³ _____." If you disagree with ⁴ _____, tell them and explain why. There's nothing wrong with disagreeing about ⁵ _____, but you can really hurt ⁶ _____ if you're unkind. If you can't discuss ⁷ _____ politely, then say ⁸ _____.

3 ⭐ (Circle) the correct pronouns.

1 She might have hurt *himself* / (*herself*) when she fell.

2 You shouldn't get annoyed with *yourself* / *ourselves* for something like this.

3 How do I look? I'm going to take a photo of *myself* / *yourself*.

4 Leticia and I met *ourselves* / *each other* at a party two years ago.

5 We really enjoyed *ourselves* / *themselves* on our vacation.

6 It was a difficult project, so they decided to help *themselves* / *one another*.

4 ⭐⭐ Underline and correct one mistake in each sentence.

1 This sport is totally safe. Anything dangerous can happen to you. ___Nothing___

2 Anna taught himself how to vlog about video games. _____

3 Phil and I are really good friends. We talk to ourselves about everything. _____

4 There isn't nothing you can do about ads on TV except switch them off. _____

5 It's nothing serious – I just cut me with a knife.
_____

6 I don't know no one at this party. Is there anyone you know here? _____

5 ⭐⭐ Complete the text with the correct indefinite or reflexive pronouns or *each other*.

My sister went to live in Canada last month to work at a big marketing company. We send messages to ¹ _each other_ almost every day, and she tells me ² _____ about her life there. She says she's enjoying ³ _____, but at first it was difficult because she didn't know ⁴ _____ in Toronto, and she had to do everything ⁵ _____ without any help. She found an apartment downtown, but there was ⁶ _____ in it – not even a bed! She lives with another girl now, but they hardly ever see ⁷ _____ because the other girl works at night. But at least she has ⁸ _____ to talk to sometimes. We all miss her!

WRITING

An Online Product Review

1 ⭐ **Read the review of an app. What does the writer particularly like about it?**

_____

2 ⭐ **Complete the _Useful Language_ phrases in the review with the words in the box.**

> allows   ~~designed~~   features   included   missing

App Reviews

| Home | News | Reviews | Top Apps | | Sign In | Register |

Search 🔍

Review: PhotoStar App

1 PhotoStar is a new app for smartphones. If you love taking photos with your phone but you think they're pretty boring, you should try this app.

2 PhotoStar is ¹ _designed_ to be used on photos on your smartphone or tablet. It ² _____ you to add funny features to your photos like emoticons, animations, and elements like glasses, beards, and funny ears. One of its best ³ _____ is that you can add voice messages using the voice of someone famous. So you can send a funny photo to your friend that has a message with your favorite celebrity's voice. I tried out all the different features and sent some photos to my friends. All of them wanted to know the name of the app. The one thing that's ⁴ _____ is a better text function so that you can also write funny messages or slogans on your photos. One is ⁵ _____ with the app, but it isn't very interesting.

3 PhotoStar is free and it has no annoying ads. It offers more features in the paid version, which is very cheap. I've recommended it to all my friends.

STAR RATING ★★★★

3 ⭐⭐ **Read the review again. In which paragraph (1–3) can you find the following?**

a a negative point ___2___

b a summary of the app ___

c a description of the app ___

d specific features of the app ___

e a recommendation ___

PLAN

4 ⭐⭐ **Choose an app to review and take notes. Think of the positive features. What do you think is missing?**

Name of app: _____

_____

A short description: _____

_____

_____

Positive features: _____

_____

_____

What's missing: _____

_____

WRITE

5 ⭐⭐⭐ **Write your review. Remember to include three paragraphs, vocabulary from the unit, and phrases from the _Useful Language_ box (see Student's Book, p101).**

CHECK

6 **Do you ...**
- give a star rating?
- say what you like and don't like about the app?
- say whether or not you would buy it?

VOCABULARY

1 Complete the sentences with the words in the box.

> ad   ad blocker   advertise   brand   buyer   influenced   logo
> marketing   product   review   seller   slogan

1 If you are not satisfied with the _____ , please return it within 15 days.

2 I can't remember the _____ name, but I know it was yellow.

3 Our company's _____ is "We work harder for you."

4 You can see the company _____ on the back of the phone.

5 Everyone loved the _____ that was shown on TV last December.

6 The products that they _____ on this website are all video games.

7 He works for a _____ company with offices all around the world.

8 A lot of children are _____ by ads on TV.

9 We found a _____ for our old car.

10 A _____ will often want to charge a higher price for the product.

11 I use an _____ so I don't see any ads on websites.

12 Bea always writes a _____ of the products she buys online.

2 Match the beginnings of the sentences 1–8 with the ends a–h.

1 On Twitter, I like following ☐
2 Dave has just posted ☐
3 If you don't want people to comment on your video, ☐
4 As an influencer, Lydia has built up ☐
5 I don't know why I subscribed ☐
6 Lately, Luke has been vlogging ☐
7 If you don't delete ☐
8 They wouldn't have shut down ☐

a you can switch that option off.

b your account if you hadn't posted those terrible things.

c about that new video game – it looks amazing.

d some photos of the party – he looks so funny.

e accounts that post information about soccer.

f that photo, I'm never going to speak to you again!

g to this channel – I don't even like rap music.

h a lot of followers since last year.

GRAMMAR IN ACTION

3 Complete the text with the correct relative pronouns.

The simplest technique [1]_____ marketing companies use to sell their products is repeating the product's name again and again. This technique, [2]_____ is most common on the radio, often doesn't explain the product. On TV, perfume companies, [3]_____ products are all very similar, use a slightly different technique, [4]_____ is to have a stunning image of a beautiful man or woman [5]_____ says the name of the brand at the end. On the Internet, [6]_____ there is often no sound, this technique is hardly ever used.

4 Complete the sentences with a reflexive pronoun or *each other.*

1 Did you hurt _____ when you dropped all those books?

2 I heard Larry talking to _____ while he was in the bathroom.

3 Diana didn't ask for help from anyone. She did everything _____ .

4 Do you and Peter see _____ every day in class?

5 When you're insecure, you have doubts about _____ and your abilities.

5 Complete the text with the indefinite pronouns in the box.

> anyone   anything   everything   nothing   someone (x2)

My friend said to me the other day that she had seen ¹_____ in an ad who looked like me. I've never been in an ad, and I don't know ²_____ who has. I watched the ad myself, and the person looked ³_____ like me at all. ⁴_____ about her was different – her hair, her face … there wasn't ⁵_____ about her that I could see that was similar to me. Maybe my friend was thinking of ⁶_____ else.

CUMULATIVE GRAMMAR

6 Complete the text with the missing words. (Circle) the correct options.

A man named Thomas J. Barratt ¹_____ to be the father of modern advertising. In 1865, Barratt started working in the Pears soap company ²_____ he created a system of advertising with works of art by ³_____ famous British painters to advertise the soap. One of the most famous paintings ⁴_____ was of a young boy, clearly from a rich family, with a bar of Pears soap in his hand – the soap ⁵_____ to the original painting. Barratt knew that ⁶_____ Pears soap in people's minds with quality would create a better image. He believed that the product ⁷_____ have a good slogan. The company used the slogan, "Good morning. Have you used Pears soap?" for well over 60 years. He also thought that if the company put Pears soap ads everywhere – in magazines, and on posters – ⁸_____ would see the ads. However, Barratt also knew that things went out of style quickly, and advertising ⁹_____ change, too. Modern advertising has kept many of Barratt's ideas, and it ¹⁰_____ his techniques ever since.

1	a considers	b considered	c has considered	d is considered
2	a which	b where	c when	d that
3	a totally	b a lot	c very	d a little
4	a used	b was using	c have used	d had used
5	a added	b had been added	c had added	d was adding
6	a connect	b connected	c connecting	d connects
7	a has to	b ought to	c must have	d can
8	a anybody	b no one	c someone	d everyone
9	a had to	b must	c could	d have to
10	a is using	b was using	c has been using	d use

9 What's new?

VOCABULARY
Reporting Verbs

1 ⭐ **Find 11 more reporting verbs in the word search.**

C	S	U	G	G	E	S	T	H	A
A	B	X	G	Y	U	W	T	K	D
P	N	P	R	O	M	I	S	E	M
O	C	N	R	A	D	E	N	Y	I
L	M	C	O	N	F	I	R	M	T
O	R	M	E	U	D	I	L	D	F
G	B	Z	Y	G	N	H	V	I	M
I	N	S	I	S	T	C	B	W	A
Z	R	E	F	U	S	E	E	J	C
E	D	I	S	C	O	V	E	R	C
E	Y	C	O	M	P	L	A	I	N
Z	N	T	D	C	L	A	I	M	A

2 ⭐⭐ **Match reporting verbs from Exercise 1 with the direct speech sentences.**

1 "No, the government is not going to close any more hospitals." *deny*

2 "Yes, it's true what you've heard. Our star player is leaving the team." _____

3 "I've told you a hundred times. I don't know who Kevin is." _____

4 "Why don't you look it up on Wikipedia?"
_____

5 "No, I'm not doing it. I'm not going shopping with you." _____

6 "I hate watching ads before videos. They're so annoying." _____

3 ⭐⭐ **Complete the story with the reporting verbs in the box. (See the *Learn to Learn* tip in the Student's Book, p107.)**

> admit   announced   ~~apologize~~   claimed
> discovered   promised

Giles had to [1] _apologize_ to all his followers for telling a big lie! On his vlog, Giles [2] _____ that he had been asked to play in a video game competition. He [3] _____ that the designers of the video game wanted him to play. At the end of his vlog, he [4] _____ to tell everyone all about it the following week. So, we waited for his vlog. Nothing happened. He didn't appear. When the competition came, we all watched, but he wasn't there either. That's when we [5] _____ that he was lying. Giles had to [6] _____ it had all been a lie. He has lost a lot of followers ... including me.

4 ⭐⭐⭐ **Write a sentence using the reporting verb and your own ideas about a time when ... .**

1 a teacher announced something
_____

2 someone refused to do something
_____

3 a friend apologized
_____

4 someone promised that they would do something for you.
_____

5 you complained about something
_____

Explore It!

Guess the correct answer.

The first 24-hour news channel was CNN, which started in ... .

a 1980   b 1995   c 2000

Find another interesting fact about a news channel or website. Write a question and send it to a classmate in an email, or ask them in the next class.

READING

A Newspaper Story

1 ⭐ **Read the newspaper story. Choose the best summary.**

  a   Police solve the mystery of "Piano Man." ⬭

  b   "Piano Man" tells his story. ⬭

  c   "Piano Man": too many questions remain. ⬭

2 ⭐⭐ **Match the underlined words in the newspaper story with the definitions.**

  1   a problem, events, or a person that is dealt with by the police   *case*

  2   strange or not understood _____

  3   a person who plays the piano _____

  4   walking slowly in no particular direction

  _____

  5   of no use or value _____

  6   very well, in a very pleasant way _____

3 ⭐⭐ **Read the story again. Answer the questions.**

  1   What was strange about the man when he was found?

    He didn't say anything.

  2   Why did the hospital think he played the piano?

  _____

  3   Why did police think he came from Norway?

  _____

  4   Why weren't they able to solve the case?

  _____

  5   How did the man get home?

  _____

  6   What is a "Hollywood ending"?

  _____

4 ⭐⭐⭐ **What do you think about this story? What was the man doing?**

_____

_____

_____

_____

The Strange <u>Case</u> of "Piano Man"

In 2005, a very strange story hit the news. Newspapers and TV stations reported that a young man had been found <u>wandering</u> the streets in a town in Kent, England. He was wearing a suit and tie, but he refused to speak.

He was taken to a hospital, and the doctors insisted that he was in good health but that he didn't speak. Then he drew a picture of a piano, so people suggested that he might be a <u>pianist</u>. A piano was taken to the hospital, and some newspapers claimed that he played the piano <u>beautifully</u> and that he seemed to be happy.

The nurses asked him where he was from, but he still didn't say anything until one day he pointed to Oslo on a map. The police announced that it was possible that he might come from Norway. They discovered that a ship had traveled from Norway to England when the man was found. Did he jump from the ship and swim to the English coast? The police asked a Norwegian speaker to talk to him, but she told them that he hadn't spoken to her either. One newspaper claimed that he wasn't able to talk at all.

TV and radio stations and newspapers asked everyone to help them to find out who the <u>mysterious</u> "Piano Man" was. Police admitted they had received a lot of calls, but all the information that people gave was <u>useless</u>.

Unfortunately, there's no Hollywood ending to this story. The man was actually Andreas Grassl, a 20-year-old from Germany, who returned there with his parents. Police discovered that he could actually talk. But what was he doing? Why was he in Kent? How did he get there? Why didn't he say anything? Why were all these stories told about him? It all remains a mystery.

GRAMMAR IN ACTION
Reported Speech: Verb Patterns

1 ⭐ (Circle) the correct option.

1 My sister told me not to *worry / worrying*.

2 She apologized *for / to* hiding the keys.

3 Hector refused to *telling / tell* me the answer.

4 Sandra insisted *for / on* going to the party.

5 I promised *to meet / meet* Karla later.

6 My parents told me *staying / to stay* home.

2 ⭐⭐ Rewrite the sentences using the correct form of the reporting verbs in the box.

> ~~admit~~   announce   deny   explain   refuse   tell

1 "All right, it was me. I dropped my drink and it fell on your bag."

Helen ___admitted that she had dropped the drink.___

2 "I'm sorry I'm late. My bike got a flat tire on the way to school."

My brother _____

3 "Look, it wasn't me. I would never send you a message like that."

David _____

4 "I'm not going to talk to Andrés ever again!"

Melanie _____

5 "Listen, everyone. Tomorrow there's going to be an exam."

The teacher _____

6 "Go home and lie down. You'll be fine in a few hours."

The doctor _____

3 ⭐ Are the sentences offers (*O*) or suggestions (*S*)?

1 I'll slice the cake in half if you like. _O_

2 Why don't you check online to see if there are any good movies out? ___

3 I can lend you a nice shirt if you need one. ___

4 I'll hold your bag while you try on the sweater. ___

5 Let's meet after class to discuss your progress. ___

6 I'll ask my dad if he can give us a ride. ___

4 ⭐⭐ Rewrite the sentences from Exercise 3. Use the reporting verbs *offered* or *suggested*.

1 Alison *offered to slice the cake in half.* ___

2 Tim _____

3 Raquel _____

4 She _____

5 The teacher _____

6 Ada _____

5 ⭐⭐⭐ Write sentences that are true for you about ....

1 something you tell your parents not to do

_____

2 something you promised a friend you would do

_____

3 a time when you denied doing something

_____

4 a suggestion you made to a friend

_____

5 something that you always refuse to do

_____

VOCABULARY AND LISTENING
Adverbs of Time and Manner

1 ⭐ Complete the sentences with the adverbs in the box.

> after a while   eventually   fluently   gradually
> nowadays   occasionally   ~~patiently~~
> regularly   secretly   surprisingly

1 I waited ____patiently____ at the movie theater for an hour, but Tim never showed up.

2 Emily only _____ posts photos on social media because she doesn't take many photos.

3 They claimed that they had _____ downloaded people's personal data without anyone knowing.

4 No one has ever heard of him in my country, but _____, he has over one million followers in Japan.

5 At first, I couldn't see anything, but _____, my eyes _____ got used to the dark, and _____, I saw the house in the distance.

6 Our French teacher speaks six languages _____, and he _____ travels to Japan because he's also learning Japanese!

7 I used to send a lot of emails but _____ I usually message people from my phone.

2 ⭐⭐ Complete the story with adverbs from Exercise 1. Sometimes more than one answer is possible.

> Paul stood beside the tree and waited
> ¹ ____patiently____ for the animal rescue people to arrive. He looked up ² _____ to check that the bird hadn't moved. It was a beautiful creature. A large eagle, Paul thought. ³ _____ the bird tried to take off, moving its wings, but not ⁴ _____, it couldn't get anywhere because one of its wings was broken. Paul ⁵ _____ wished he could speak bird language ⁶ _____, to tell it that everything would be fine. ⁷ _____, a white van arrived. A man and woman got out. They approached the bird ⁸ _____ so as not to scare it. The woman threw a blanket over it, and they ⁹ _____ managed to get it into a cage. When they had gone, Paul walked home looking at the photos on his phone.

A Radio Interview

🎧 **3** ⭐ Listen to an interview about viral videos. Which of these reasons does the man <u>not</u> give for why we share a video?
9.01

It's useful.   ☐

It causes positive or negative feelings.   ☐

It makes us laugh.   ☐

It's important to us.   ☐

It has a story.   ☐

🎧 **4** ⭐⭐ Listen again. Complete the notes with key words and information.
9.01

1 Jonah Cook is a _marketing manager_.

2 There are _____ things you need to do to communicate well.

3 We like to watch a good story until _____ to find out what happens.

4 "How-to" videos are _____ because they help us do something.

5 There are a lot of videos with _____ that show you how to build up followers.

6 We share "how-to" videos because it makes us look _____.

5 ⭐⭐⭐ Send your answers to Exercise 4 to a friend in an email and compare them. (See the *Learn to Learn* tip in the Student's Book, p110.)

GRAMMAR IN ACTION
Reported Questions

1 ⭐ **Complete the reported questions with one word in each blank.**

1 My teacher asked me where I ___was___ going.
2 She asked me _____ I was chatting with.
3 The coach asked me what my favorite sport _____ .
4 Nicolas asked me _____ I wanted something to eat, but I told him I wasn't hungry.
5 Molly wanted to know if I _____ gone to the party last Friday.
6 Juan asked me if he _____ come to my house to watch the game later.

2 ⭐⭐⭐ **Rewrite the reported questions from Exercise 1 in direct speech.**

1 "___Where are you going___?" my teacher asked me.
2 "_____?" she asked.
3 "_____?" the coach asked.
4 "_____?" Nicolas asked. I told him I wasn't hungry.
5 "_____?" Molly asked.
6 "_____?" Ean asked me.

3 ⭐⭐ **Put the words in the correct order to make reported questions.**

1 was / where / asked / the station / We / a police officer

We asked a police officer where the station was.

2 asked / My / been / I'd / where / dad / me

_____

3 help / Paul / I / his / bike / me / if / asked / could / fix / him

_____

4 tomorrow / to school / ask / me / if / She / didn't / I / was / going

_____

5 asked / Marco / me / I'd / Brooke / seen / when

_____

Indirect Questions

4 ⭐⭐ **Complete the interview with a famous rock star. Rewrite the underlined questions as indirect questions.**

A Thanks for talking to me, Jimmy B. First, [1] <u>what was your favorite subject in school?</u>

Can _you tell me what your favorite subject in_ _school was_ ?

B Sure. It was math.

A [2] <u>Why did you start playing the guitar?</u>

Would you mind _____

_____?

B My dad had a guitar, so I just decided to pick it up one day.

A [3] <u>Are you happy with your latest album?</u>

Could _____

_____?

B Yes, I'm very happy with it. It's my best album so far.

A [4] <u>When is your next tour?</u>

Do _____

_____?

B It will start next spring.

5 ⭐⭐⭐ **Think about questions you have asked this week. Write them as indirect questions.**

Would you mind telling me when our report is due?

_____

_____

_____

_____

WRITING
A News Story

1 ⭐ **Read the news story. How do the children communicate in the village of Ubang?**

_____

2 ⭐ **Match the sentences 1–5 with the paragraphs A–C.**

1 an expert's explanation of the Ubang languages   [B]
2 an explanation given by the Ubang chief   [ ]
3 a fear about the future   [ ] and [ ]
4 a general belief about communication between men and women   [ ]
5 examples of different words that Ubang men and women have for things   [ ]

3 ⭐⭐ **Complete the *Useful Language* phrases in the news story with the words in the box.**

> asked   explained that   nowadays   said   ~~surprisingly~~

What Did You Say?

A People, especially older people, often complain that men and women don't understand each other. But there is a Nigerian village where men and women actually do speak different languages because, ¹ _surprisingly_ , they use different vocabularies for many things. Ubang people are proud of their language and culture but are afraid that the language will not continue.

B In the village of Ubang, women use the words *okwakwe* for "dog" and *ogbala* for "cup," and men say *abu* and *nko*. And there are many other examples of words that sound different and use completely different letters. When ² _____ if men and women find it difficult to understand each other, the Ubang village chief ³ _____ everyone understands each other perfectly and that they are very proud of the difference. In fact, there are a lot of words that men and women have in common. Ms. Chi Chi Undie, who has studied the community, says that the men and women of the tribe live very separate lives. "All their children are brought up speaking the women's language fluently," she ⁴ _____ . When the boys get older, they learn to speak like the men in order to be closer to them.

C ⁵ _____ , most children are learning English, and the older members of the community ask what is going to happen to their unique language situation. … The village chief is determined that it will survive because, he says, "if the languages die, the Ubang people will exist no more."

PLAN

4 Write a news story. First, research a current news story on a few websites to get different versions. Take notes on these things in your notebook.
- A general introduction
- The basic facts of the story (who? what? where?)
- An interesting fact or extra information
- Quotes from the people involved

WRITE

5 Write your story. Remember to include three paragraphs, language from this unit, and phrases from the *Useful Language* box (see Student's Book, p113).

CHECK

6 Do you …
- include an interesting headline?
- include some extra details in the third paragraph?
- include some direct speech?

VOCABULARY

1 Complete the sentences. The first letter is given.

1 Sarah s_____ that we buy a present for James.

2 I said he was lying, and he a_____ I was right.

3 Julia c_____ she met Lionel Messi, but I don't believe her.

4 Remember that you p_____ to help me move my bed later.

5 The students are c_____ that the classroom is too cold.

6 Francesca d_____ that she had fallen asleep in class, but everyone could see her.

7 The president a_____ that he was going to visit our school.

8 Ricardo still hasn't a_____ for breaking my watch.

9 The teacher o_____ to let Sophie take the exam again.

10 Thomas has always i_____ that nobody told him about the trip to France.

11 I can't believe that you are r_____ to talk to Victoria because she lost your sweater.

12 The school principal c_____ that the art teacher had had an accident.

2 Circle the correct adverbs to complete the sentences.

1 Isaac *patiently / secretly* hid the box, and nobody knows where it is.

2 I only *gradually / occasionally* clean my computer. I should do it more often.

3 They waited *patiently / eventually* in line for hours, but there were no tickets left.

4 My dad has a friend who speaks eight languages *nowadays / fluently*!

5 I saved ten dollars every week, and *regularly / gradually*, I saved enough money for a new phone.

6 *After a while / Nowadays*, hardly anyone sends letters to people.

7 The doctor says that my dad should exercise more *regularly / occasionally*.

8 The movie was interesting at the beginning, but *secretly / after a while*, I got bored and fell asleep.

9 I thought the food would be pretty ordinary, but it was *surprisingly / patiently* delicious.

10 Mark sent a message to say he was late, and *eventually / gradually*, he arrived at 11:30.

GRAMMAR IN ACTION

3 Match the beginnings of the sentences 1–7 with the endings a–g.

1 We asked the teacher if ☐   a I was doing later.

2 The police told everyone ☐   b that I had to remember the card I had in my hand.

3 Lucas asked me what ☐   c to clear the area because there was a big fire.

4 My parents suggested ☐   d to help me fix my bike.

5 Beatrice offered ☐   e where this street goes?

6 The magician explained ☐   f we had to write in pen or pencil.

7 Could you tell me ☐   g going to the beach for the weekend.

4 Complete the second sentence so that it reports the first. Use no more than three words.

1 "Can you look it up on the Internet?" Ivan asked me.

Ivan asked me _____ look it up on the Internet.

2 "What did Josh say in the message?" Sara asked her.

Sara asked her what _____ in the message.

3 "Would you mind inviting me next time?" I asked Ann.

I asked Ann _____ next time.

4 "Where are you waiting for me?" asked Bella.

Bella asked me _____ waiting for her.

5 "How did you know the answer?" Leo asked us.

Leo asked us _____ the answer.

6 "Do you need directions to the station?" asked the police officer.

The police officer asked us _____ directions to the station.

CUMULATIVE GRAMMAR

5 Complete the text with the missing words. (Circle) the correct options.

SCIENCE NEWS: Goats Prefer Happy Faces

Everyone loves a happy animal, [1]_____? Scientists in England [2]_____ that goats are attracted more by happy faces than by angry ones. It suggests that goats, like other animals [3]_____ humans keep at home or on farms, [4]_____ read human faces and understand human feelings. Previous studies had [5]_____ shown similar results in tests [6]_____ were done with horses and dogs.

In the tests, the reactions of the goats were studied by [7]_____ them in a closed area. Then different faces [8]_____ to people who gave them pasta to eat, [9]_____ is their favorite snack. The goats went to the happy faces more often and spent [10]_____ more time studying the faces with their noses. They also found that if they changed the faces from men to women, it [11]_____ any difference to the goats. Scientists believe the results [12]_____ us understand animals better in the future.

1	a doesn't it	b does he	c don't I	d don't they
2	a just have discovered	b have discovered just	c have just discovered	d have just discover
3	a what	b that	c if	d to
4	a can	b should	c ought to	d can't
5	a still	b never	c yet	d already
6	a who	b that	c where	d whose
7	a put	b to put	c putting	d puts
8	a attached	b are attached	c were attaching	d were attached
9	a which	b what	c that	d who
10	a really	b a lot	c fairly	d totally
11	a makes	b would make	c didn't make	d hadn't made
12	a were helped	b help	c helped	d will help

EXAM TIPS: Listening Skills

Listening: Multiple-Choice Pictures

You will listen to short extracts and choose from different options. This tests your ability to listen for specific information and answer questions about what you hear.

Exam Guide: Multiple Choice

- If the question is about a conversation between a boy and a girl, <u>underline</u> which of the two people you need to answer the question about. For example: *What food will <u>the boy</u> eat?*

- Decide if the question is asking about the past, present, or future. The verb tense and time expressions in the question will help you. For example: *What is the weather like now?* is a completely different question from *What will the weather be like tomorrow?*

- Listen carefully to see if the meaning is positive or negative. For example: *Can you buy some fruit – but not bananas?* tells us that the speaker does not want bananas.

- Usually the answer will come in the middle or at the end of the listening and not at the beginning. This means that you should always wait until the end of each listening before you choose your answer.

REMEMBER!

Don't choose a picture as an answer just because you hear information about it in the listening. Usually you will hear information related to all three pictures!

Listening Practice: Multiple-Choice Pictures

Tip!
Listen for key words and synonyms to help you identify the answer.

1 **Choose the correct meaning for the expressions.**

1 Are you kidding me?

   A I don't believe you.   B That's interesting!

2 You're getting on my nerves.

   A You're funny!   B You're irritating me!

3 You'll never know unless you try.

   A You should try.   B Are you going to try?

4 You're coming to my party, aren't you?

   A Are you sure you're coming to my party?

   B Can you confirm that you're coming to my party?

5 You must feel really proud of your exam results!

   A I'm sure you feel really happy about your exam results.

   B You ought to feel very happy about your exam results.

6 I get a lot out of playing chess.

   A Playing chess is hard for me.   B I really enjoy playing chess.

🎧 **2** **You will hear six short extracts. Are the sentences _T_ (true) or _F_ (false)?**
E.01

1 The boy's sister irritates the girl. ___

2 The speaker says everyone should study abroad. ___

3 The boy's coffee is very hot. ___

4 There is a present in the box. ___

5 Some fruit tastes better than it smells. ___

6 The girl thinks going to college is a bad idea. ___

.... **Tip!**

Sometimes information later in the listening will contradict or correct the information before. For example:

A _Amy loves skateboarding._

B _Well, that was before her accident. She hasn't done it since then._

This is another reason why you need to wait until the end before choosing your answer.

🎧 **3** **Listen to the conversation between Ben and his mom.**
E.02 **Answer _Yes_ or _No_.**

1 Are the dishes washed? _____

2 Does Ben need to do his homework tonight? _____

3 Is Ben going to speak to his friends tonight? _____

🎧 **4** **Listen again. What is Ben going to do first? Choose the correct option A, B, or C.**
E.02

Ⓐ

Ⓑ

Ⓒ

EXAM TIPS: Reading Skills

Matching People with Activities and Things

You will read descriptions of people and match them with the best options. Remember that there are more options than people, so read carefully! The extra options usually fit only partially, not completely.

Exam Guide: Multiple Matching

- Begin by reading the five descriptions of the people. <u>Underline</u> the key information in each description.
- Next, read all eight texts carefully and <u>underline</u> the key information in each one.
- Then compare the <u>underlined</u> information in the description of the first person with the <u>underlined</u> information in the texts. Which text is the best match for this person?
- Don't choose a text just because it repeats some words from the description of one person. You need to focus on the meaning of the descriptions and the texts and not on individual words.

REMEMBER!

Be very careful when choosing – the text needs to be <u>a perfect match for everything the person wants</u>.

Reading Practice: Multiple Matching

Identifying Meaning

1 **Choose the option (A, B, or C) that shows the meaning of the first sentence.**

   1 Jack wants to do without chocolate for a week.

     A Jacks wants to eat less chocolate for seven days.

     B Jack thinks he can do without chocolate for seven days.

     C Jack would like not to eat chocolate for seven days.

   2 Chloe is looking forward to learning to drive.

     A Chloe plans to learn to drive.

     B Chloe is happy that she will start learning to drive soon.

     C In the future, Chloe will learn to drive.

   3 Liam has moved to Veracruz.

     A Liam is living in Veracruz now.

     B Liam has traveled to Veracruz.

     C Liam is spending some time in Veracruz.

Synonyms

2 **Match the <u>underlined</u> words with the synonyms in the box. There are four extra words.**

> be born   can   cook in oil   cook in an oven   cut into pieces
> heat   know   lived as a child   think   will possibly

1 I'm going to <u>bake</u> a cake. _____
2 Jon <u>grew up</u> in Chicago. _____
3 How long does it take to <u>fry</u> the onions? _____
4 Rachel <u>might</u> go to college. _____
5 I <u>guess</u> they must be brother and sister. _____
6 You need to <u>chop</u> the peppers. _____

Tip!
Don't look for words that match exactly. Read the text carefully and <u>underline</u> synonyms of the key information words.

Eliminating Options

3 **Read what Laura wants. Then decide which options A–D you can eliminate.**

Laura wants to buy a new phone. It must be the latest model, feel very light and smooth, and have a very large display.

A We repair all the latest models of phones …
B Our store has a good selection of phones, including classic old models …
C We have the latest models. They're very light, and have big displays. We're definitely the best place to get a new watch.
D This store specializes in all sorts of digital devices. Its products are expensive, but they look great!

Tip!
When you think you have a correct answer, check the incorrect options again to be sure that they don't match.

Finding Differences

4 **Read about Sam and Nathan. Find three differences between them.**

Sam wants to try out some new recipes. He cooks every day. During the week, he doesn't have much time to cook, but he has time on the weekend to make more complicated dishes. He doesn't eat fried food or food with a very strong flavor.

Nathan likes very spicy food. He wants to buy a book of recipes. He is especially interested in making quick meals in the frying pan.

_____
_____
_____

EXAM TIPS: Listening Skills

Listening: Fill in the Blanks

You'll have to listen and complete notes or sentences. The notes or sentences summarize what you hear. You have to write a word, number, or very short noun phrase in each blank.

Exam guide: Fill in the Blanks

- Pay attention to the instructions. They remind you what you have to do, but more importantly, they tell you what the topic is.
- After the instructions, there is a pause. Use this to read the notes or sentences.
- While you read, try to think about what type of information is missing. It might be a day, a number, a date, or a price, for example.
- The sentences or notes summarize what the speaker says, so you are not going to hear what is written on the page. Pay attention to the key words.
- As you listen, fill in the blanks – remember the answers are one word, a number, or a very short phrase.
- During the second listening, check your answers.

REMEMBER!

Check that your answers make sense in the context if you are given a second opportunity to listen.

Tip!

The sentences and notes will give you clues about what type of information is missing. Read everything carefully.

LISTENING PRACTICE: Fill in the Blanks

1 **Read the notes. What type of information is missing?**

> <u>Rent a Bus</u>
> Number of seats on our bus: ¹_____
> Bus leaves: 10:30 a.m.
> Meet at youth club: ²_____
> Price of exhibition entrance: $7
> Special group price (over 20 people): ³$_____

🎧 2 **You will hear some information about a visit to a photography**
E.03 **exhibition. Listen and write the correct answer in the blanks (1–3)**
in Exercise 1. Then listen again and write down the other numbers
that you hear.

_____

Tip!

What you read in the questions is not what the person says – it is a summary or paraphrase. Think about the meaning and listen for key words.

🎧 **3** **Listen and complete the sentences.**
E.04

    A Angela's mom told her that her _____ had won the contest many years ago.

    B To find out more about the contest, visit the website – www_____org.

    C Angela entered the contest with her _____ .

    D The class was given a grant of $ _____ to build their robot.

4 **You will hear an announcement about events coming up at a youth club. Before you listen, read the notes in Exercise 5. What type of information is missing from the blanks?**

> a type of clothing   a day   the name of a food   a number   a subject   a time

🎧 **5** **Listen and complete the notes with one or two words or a number, date, or time.**
E.05

Youth Club Events: November

Weekly cooking classes:

Every [1]_____ at 5 p.m.

Mary

1) bake a chocolate cake; 2) roast [2]_____

Visit 1:

Date: Friday, the 16th at [3]_____ p.m.

Helen Fields – fashion designer

Workshop: match colors; choose jeans; decorate a plain white [4]_____ (must bring)

Visit 2:

Date: Saturday, the 24th at 7 p.m.

Dr. Michael Redding – professor of [5]_____

Talk: history of logos

Logo contest:

1st prize [6]$_____ in cash

GRAMMAR REFERENCE

STARTER

Past and Present, Simple and Continuous

- We use the **simple present** to talk about facts, habits, and routines.
  My sister likes pizza.
  I don't read every day.

- We use the **simple past** to talk about completed events and actions in the past.
  I translated the text into Spanish for him.
  I visited Madrid three years ago.

- We use the **present continuous** to talk about actions that are happening now or around now.
  That girl over there is waving at me.

- We use the **past continuous** to talk about actions in progress around a time in the past. We also use **when** and **while** to mean "during that time," or to connect two events happening at the same time.
  Isabella was wearing a dress last night.
  While I was looking for the dog, he was looking for the ball.

Present Perfect and Simple Past

- We use the **present perfect** when something started or happened in the past and continues to be true until now. We can say how long something has been true but not when it started.
  I've been to Barcelona. (When isn't specified, but it continues to be true.)
  They've been sightseeing. (We don't know when.)
  She's wanted to talk to you since she arrived. (She continues to want to.)

- We use the **simple past** when the moment in which something happened has ended. When it happened isn't always mentioned, usually because it is clear.
  I went to Barcelona in June.
  They went sightseeing yesterday.
  She wanted to talk to you.

86 GRAMMAR REFERENCE & PRACTICE

GRAMMAR PRACTICE

Past and Present, Simple and Continuous

1 (Circle) the correct options.

1 I (cut) / *was cutting* my finger yesterday.

2 *Do you go / Are you going* to the supermarket now?

3 What *happens / is happening* when you push this button?

4 Mary *listened / was listening* to music when I *saw / was seeing* her.

5 You *don't need / aren't needing* to pack a lot of clothes.

6 *Did you buy / Were you buying* some bread for a sandwich?

2 Complete the conversation with the correct form of the verbs in parentheses.

MOM Harry, you're going to be late. What
¹ _____are you doing_____ (you / do)?

HARRY I ² _____ (try) to find my keys!

MOM Where ³ _____ (you / normally / leave) them?

HARRY I always ⁴_____ (put) them on my desk. But they're not there now.

MOM When ⁵_____ (you / have) them last?

HARRY I ⁶_____ (have) them in my hand when I ⁷_____ (arrive) here yesterday. I ⁸_____ (talk) to Jonah on the phone.

MOM Oh, yes, I ⁹_____ (remember). You ¹⁰_____ (go) into the living room.

HARRY I ¹¹_____ (look) there, but I ¹² _____ (not find) them.

MOM ¹³_____ (you / wear) your coat?

HARRY Yes, I was. Maybe I ¹⁴_____ (leave) them in my coat pocket. Here they are!

Present Perfect and Simple Past

3 Complete the sentences with the present perfect or simple past form of the verbs in the box.

not laugh   not play   paint   ~~see~~   sing   tell

1 ___Have___ you ___seen___ Scarlett? She's looking for you.

2 Pete _____ very well at the concert yesterday.

3 I _____ you 100 times! Don't call me Timmy!

4 Don't touch the door. They _____ just _____ it.

5 Why _____ you _____ at that joke? It was really funny.

6 Lucas _____ soccer for a month. He's injured.

4 Put the words in the correct order to make sentences.

1 sent / Has / photo / you / Erin / the / ?
   Has Erin sent you the photo?

2 tennis / I / liked / you / didn't / know / playing / .
   _____

3 long / your / taken / a / You / time / to / essay / have / finish / .
   _____
   _____

4 questions / the / didn't / exam / all / answer / on / the / We / .
   _____
   _____

5 you / us / did / Why / come / with / to / decide / ?
   _____

6 heard / from / We / news / Julia / any / haven't / .
   _____

Present Perfect Simple

- We use the **present perfect** to talk about actions, experiences, and facts in the past when the exact time is not mentioned or important.
I've found my favorite T-shirt.
She has been to the mall.

Present Perfect Continuous

	Affirmative	Negative
He / She / It	has been practicing for years.	hasn't been eating very well.
I / We / You / They	have been practicing for years.	haven't been eating very well.

Questions		
Has	he / she / it	been sleeping a lot?
Have	I / we / you / they	

Short Answers		
Yes,	he / she / it	has.
	I / we / you / they	have.
No,	he / she / it	hasn't.
	I / we / you / they	haven't.

- We use the **present perfect continuous** to talk about an action or a series of actions that started in the past, is still in progress, and we expect to continue.
I've been studying hard all week.
She's been exercising since last summer.

- We often use the **present perfect continuous** to say how long we have been doing something.
I've been taking piano lessons for nine years.

- We use the **present perfect continuous** to focus on the ongoing action rather than the result.
We've been preparing for the party all day!

- We don't use the **present perfect continuous** with stative verbs (e.g., *like, have,* and *know*).
Emily has liked him since she met him.
(NOT *Emily has been liking him since she met him.*)
We have had our cat since she was a kitten.
(NOT *We've been having our cat since she was a kitten.*)

- We form the **present perfect continuous** with **subject** + **has/have** (**not**) + **been** + **-ing**.
I've been playing basketball since I was seven.
She's sick, so she hasn't been coming to school this week.

- We form **present perfect continuous** questions with **has/have** + **subject** + **been** + **-ing**.
Has she been living here for a long time?

Present Perfect Simple and Present Perfect Continuous

- We use the **present perfect simple** to emphasize that the action or event is recently finished. We use the **present perfect continuous** for actions or events that are still going on up to now.
I've studied for my English test tomorrow.
(completed action)
I've been studying for my English test tomorrow.
(ongoing)

Modifiers

- We use **modifiers** with adjectives to make the meaning stronger and show emphasis. Common modifiers include *a bit, a little, a lot, totally, really, absolutely, extremely, pretty, fairly,* and *far.*
He was really upset.
I felt extremely sorry for him.
Her parents are pretty strict.
She can't do anything.
They work extremely hard.
They need to relax.
Her room is really messy.
There's stuff everywhere!

GRAMMAR PRACTICE

Present Perfect Simple

1 Complete the sentences with the present perfect simple form of the verbs in parentheses.

1 I ___haven't worn___ (not wear) this dress since last spring!

2 Paul _____ (wait) all his life for this moment.

3 _____ Jane _____ (tell) you what happened yesterday?

4 We _____ (not play) this computer game for months.

5 Our school _____ (organize) a fashion show.

Present Perfect Continuous

2 Complete the sentences with the present perfect continuous form of the verbs in the box.

> clean ~~listen~~ rain run wear

1 I ___'ve been listening___ to this great radio station on my phone.

2 Your face is red. _____ you _____ ?

3 It _____ all morning, so we can't go out.

4 Her feet hurt because she _____ those high-heeled boots all day.

5 Vanessa _____ her room all morning – it was a mess!

Present Perfect Simple and Present Perfect Continuous

3 (Circle) the correct options.

1 How many times have you (seen) / been seeing this movie?

2 I've folded / been folding all my clothes, and they're in my suitcase now.

3 Have you sent / been sending the photos to me yet?

4 Dad's tired because he has painted / been painting all day.

5 Daniel hasn't read / been reading Laura's message yet, so don't tell him what she said.

6 I've ordered / been ordering pizza – it'll be here in a few minutes.

4 Complete the conversation with the present perfect simple or continuous form of the verbs in parentheses.

TIM Hi, Mia. I [1] ___haven't seen___ (not see) you all day. What [2] _____ (you / do)?

MIA Oh, hi, Tim. I [3] _____ (study) for an exam. It's history. I [4] _____ (always / find) it hard to study history.

TIM Me, too. I [5] _____ (even / not start) yet. I [6] _____ (try) to write that essay for English class. I [7] _____ (not finish) it yet, though.

MIA I have. Do you want to see it? I [8] _____ (write) about my last vacation. I'm really happy with it.

TIM That's funny. I [9] _____ (do) the same thing. Maybe the teacher's going to think we [10] _____ (copy) each other!

Modifiers

5 (Circle) the correct options.

1 I'm not buying these jeans. They're absolutely / (much too) big for me.

2 The movie was really / totally good and a bit / extremely funny.

3 Lydia's dress was totally / a lot amazing, and her brother looked pretty / a little handsome.

4 These jeans are a bit / pretty shorter than those jeans.

6 Match the beginnings with the endings.

1 The exam was really

2 I'm really

3 Diego thought the story was fairly

4 Edwin's party was a lot more

5 Liam takes totally amazing

6 The food was pretty

a fun than Carl's party last month.

b good, but I didn't like the music.

c sorry, but I can't talk now.

d amusing, but nobody else liked it.

e difficult, but I think I passed.

f photos, but he never shares them.

Used To, Would, and Simple Past

- **Used to** emphasizes that past states, habits, and actions are now finished.
  It used to be a castle, but now it's a museum.
  She used to play piano. Nowadays, she just sings.

- **Used to** does not have a present form. For present habits and states, we use the simple present.
  My cousin visits us every summer.
  (NOT ~~My cousin use to visit us every summer.~~)

- We use **used to** and **would** to talk about habits and actions in the past that are different today.
  They used to run on Tuesdays, but now they run on Fridays.
  When I was young, my parents would take me for a walk every day.

- We also use **used to**, but not **would**, to talk about states and feelings in the past that are different today.
  My grandfather used to have black hair, but now it's white.
  (NOT ~~My grandfather would have black hair …~~)
  She used to love volleyball, but she doesn't play anymore.
  (NOT ~~She would love volleyball …~~)

- We do not use **used to** or **would** to talk about things that only happened once or to say how many times something happened.
  Last year, I went to Mexico.
  (NOT ~~Last year, I used to go to Mexico.~~)
  Yesterday, I called my dad three times.
  (NOT ~~Yesterday, I would call my dad three times.~~)

- We put question words at the beginning of the question.
  What things did you use to do when you were younger?

- We don't often use **would** in questions and negative sentences.

- **Used to** is like any regular verb. The past tense ends in **d**, but in questions and negative forms, the verb does not end in **d**.
  I used to like playing, but I didn't use to like practicing.
  Did you use to have a bike when you were younger?

Past Perfect with Never, Ever, Already, By (Then), By the Time

- We use the **past perfect** with other past tenses to talk about actions or states that happened before the main past action or state.
  We hadn't seen the news, so we didn't know about the storms.
  I couldn't call you on Friday because I had left my phone at home.

- We use **adverbs** and **adverbial phrases** such as *already, never, ever, by the time,* and *by then* with the past perfect.

- **Already**, **never**, and **ever** come before the past participle, but **yet** comes at the end of the sentence.
  We had never been to New York until last year.
  They've gone to school, but they haven't had breakfast yet.

- We use **already** to emphasize that something had happened.
  I had already finished my test before class was over.

- If something had happened **by the time** something else happened, it happened before it.
  They had already heard the news by the time I told them.

- If something had happened **by then**, it happened before then.
  I finally arrived at the party, but by then all the food had gone.

GRAMMAR PRACTICE

Used To, Would, and Simple Past

1 Complete the sentences with *used to* and the verbs in parentheses.

1 I _didn't use to like_ (not like) wearing dresses when I was younger.

2 Edwin _____ (eat) a lot of candy until his dentist told him to stop.

3 Adela _____ (not look) forward to PE classes because she wasn't very fit.

4 Our soccer team _____ (win) every game, but now they're terrible!

5 My dad _____ (not have) a cell phone when he was 15.

6 My teachers _____ (not give) us much homework.

2 Make questions with *used to* or the simple past. Sometimes both are possible.

1 When / Helen / buy / this car / ?

When did Helen buy this car?

2 there / always / be / a movie theater here / ?

_____

3 your dad / have / a bike / when he was a teenager / ?

_____

4 you / hear / what happened yesterday / ?

_____

5 What types of music / you / listen to / when you were younger / ?

_____

3 Choose the correct sentences. Sometimes both are correct.

1 a When she younger, my aunt used to live in Miami.
  b When she was younger, my aunt would live in Miami.

2 a When I was five, I wouldn't eat vegetables.
  b When I was five, I didn't use to eat vegetables.

3 a There used to be a lot more stores on this street.
  b There would be a lot more stores on this street.

4 a My dad used to have a long beard.
  b My dad would have a long beard.

Past Perfect with *Never, Ever, Already, By (Then), By the Time*

4 Circle the correct options.

1 I was excited because I'd never / already been to a wedding before.

2 Had the teacher *already / never* started the class when Paul arrived?

3 By *then / the time* you called, it was too late to do anything.

4 When the movie started, they'd *never / already* eaten all the pizza.

5 I started running, but *by then / by the time,* the man had disappeared.

6 When we took my grandmother to Los Angeles, she had *never / ever* flown before.

5 Complete the text with the words in the box.

already   by   had   had already   ~~never~~   then

I was very nervous. I'd ¹ _never_ played the guitar in front of people before. I walked onto the stage. ² _____ the time I'd picked up the guitar, my hands were shaking. They ³ _____ turned the lights off, so I couldn't really see much. I put the strap around my neck, but by ⁴ _____, the rest of the band had ⁵ _____ started playing the first song! I put my hands on the guitar to play … and there was no sound. Someone ⁶ _____ pulled the plug!

6 Use the prompts to write simple past and past perfect sentences.

1 They / not sleep / all night because / there / be / a big storm

They hadn't slept all night because there was a big storm.

2 By the time we / get / there, our team / score

_____

3 I / try / to cancel my order yesterday, but by then, / they / already send / it

_____

4 Until last week, Camilla / never / speak / in English

_____

5 When you / arrive, / Dennis / already / find / his keys

_____

Future Forms

- We use **be going to** to talk about future plans and intentions and predictions that we feel sure about.
  After I graduate, I'm going to travel the world.
  My sister is going to stay with my grandparents this summer.
  I'm going to feel sick if I eat all of that!

- We use **will** to talk about what is going to happen in the future, especially things that you are certain about or things that are planned.
  I'll see him tomorrow.
  I won't cook later – I'll be out.

- We use **may** (**not**) or **might** (**not**) instead of **will** (**not**) to show that we feel less sure about a future action or event but think it is probable.
  I might not go to college.
  I may get a job with my dad.
  When he gets here, he may want to speak to you.
  Don't call after ten o'clock – we may be watching a movie.

Present Continuous for Future

- We use the **present continuous** to talk about future arrangements when the time is fixed.
  They're getting married this summer.
  What are you doing this weekend? – I'm going shopping with my parents.
  She isn't coming to the party. She's spending the day with her cousins.

Simple Present for Future

- We use the **simple present** to talk about events that are scheduled or timetabled.
  The lesson starts at 9:30 tomorrow instead of 10:30.
  They don't go back to school until next Monday.

Future Continuous

Affirmative/Negative		
I / You / He / She / It / We / You / They	will	be flying this time next week.
I / You / He / She / It / We / You / They	won't	

Questions		
Will	I / you / he / she / it / we / you / they	be flying this time next week?

Short Answers		
Yes,	I / you / he / she / it / we / you / they	will.
No,	I / you / he / she / it / we / you / they	won't.

- We form the **future continuous** with **will/may/might** + **be** + **-ing**.
- We use the **future continuous** to talk about actions we believe will be in progress at a future time.
  In five years, he'll be living in Veracruz and working as a teacher.
  By 2025, everyone will be wearing smartwatches.
- We can also use the **future continuous** to talk about future plans.
  I'll be leaving at 2 p.m. I'm picking my little brother up from school, so I can't be late.
- We put question words at the beginning of a question.
  What will you be doing in 20 years?
  When will computers be cooking dinner for us?

Future Perfect

Affirmative/Negative		
I / You / He / She / It / We / You / They	will have finished	the project by 2050.
I / You / He / She / It / We / You / They	won't have finished	

Questions		
Will	I / you / he / she / it / we / you / they	have finished	the project by 2050?

Short Answers		
Yes,	I / you / he / she / it / we / you / they	will.
No,	I / you / he / she / it / we / you / they	won't.

- We form the **future perfect** with **will** + **have** + **past participle**.
- We use the **future perfect** for actions that will be completed before a certain time in the future.

Future Forms

1 Circle the correct options.

1 Mike's not sure yet, but he *'s going to* / *might* get a new bike.

2 Do you think it *'s going to* / *might* be a sunny day tomorrow?

3 Some scientists say the world's temperature *will* / *going to* rise by four degrees in the next ten years.

4 Enjoy your vacation. I'm sure you *'ll* / *might* have a great time.

5 Tracy is certain she *is going to* / *might* study biology in college. It's her favorite subject.

6 I'm not feeling very well, so I *may not* / *won't* go to the game. I'll text you later.

2 Complete the sentences with the correct future form of the verbs in parentheses.

1 This restaurant _____doesn't open_____ (not open) until 5 p.m. this evening.

2 Do you think you _____ (pass) all your classes?

3 What time _____ (Tim / meet) us tomorrow?

4 I've decided I _____ (not buy) a new printer.

5 Larry hasn't decided yet, but he _____ (not have) dinner with us.

6 I _____ (order) pizza at the restaurant tonight.

3 Complete the conversations with the correct form of the verbs in the box.

> buy   need   ~~overcook~~   start

1 **A** Can I help you with dinner?
  B Yes. You fry the chicken because I __'ll__ probably _____overcook_____ it!

2 **A** Where are you going?
  B Into town. I _____ a new coat.

3 **A** What time do you want to meet?
  B The concert _____ at 8 p.m., so let's say 7:30.

4 **A** Is there enough food for everyone?
  B I don't know. I think we _____ more bread.

Future Continuous and Future Perfect

4 Complete the sentences with the future continuous form of the verbs in parentheses.

1 What ___will you be doing___ (you / do) this time tomorrow?

2 My jeans are dirty, so I _____ (not wear) them tomorrow.

3 The music teacher says she _____ (not teach) us how to play this song.

4 While you're working hard, I _____ (enjoy) myself on vacation.

5 You can't meet him later; you _____ (write) your English essay.

6 Tomorrow's a national holiday, so we _____ (prepare) a special meal!

5 Complete the text with the future perfect form of the verbs in the box.

> drink   eat   laugh   see   ~~sleep~~   spend

What do humans do in one year? By this time next year, you [1] __will have slept__ for 2,372 hours and you [2] _____ over 1,000 hours on the Internet. You [3] _____ probably _____ some funny things, which means you [4] _____ for a total of 36.5 hours. If you're American, you [5] _____ around 46 slices of pizza, and you [6] _____ probably _____ well over 800 liters of water.

6 Correct the mistake in each sentence.

1 This time tomorrow, I'll ~~have~~ lying on the beach in Italy. _____be_____

2 In 20 years, we'll be built robots to do the cooking for us. _____

3 By the time tomorrow, I'll have finished all my exams. _____

4 I be not doing anything later, so call me.
  _____

5 Will have you started dinner when I get home?
  _____

6 What will be you wearing to Itzel's party?
  _____

Modals of Deduction and Possibility

- We often use **can**, **can't**, **could**, **may**, **might**, and **must** + **infinitive without to** to say how possible or probable we think an action or event is.
  It can't be him! He never wears a hat to a party!
  She's late. She might be stuck in traffic.
  You must be tired after your long trip.

- We use **can** to make general statements about possibilities.
  They say that drinking too much coffee can be bad for you.
  Try drinking more water; it can help you feel more awake!

- We use **can't** to say that we think something is impossible or cannot be true.
  That can't be Samantha. She's in China!
  They can't be at home. I saw them leaving an hour ago.

- We use **could**, **may**, and **might** to say we think something is possible.
  You could have an infection; that's why you're feeling bad.
  A *Who's that man?*
  B *I don't know. He may be her husband.*
  It might be cold outside, so I'll take a coat.

- We use **must** when we think something is highly probable.
  She's not answering her phone. She must be busy.

Obligation, Prohibition, Necessity, and Advice

- We use **must** and **have to** to say that it is necessary to do something.
  Visitors must complete the form and then give it to the receptionist.
  We have to fill in this form and then send it to the office.

- We often use **must** when the obligation comes from the speaker – it's something the speaker considers important.
  You must do your homework before you go to Greg's house.
  I must get my grandfather a present for his birthday. I forgot last year!

- **Must** is followed by an infinitive without *to*.

- We use **have to** to say what it is necessary to do.
  You have to answer all the questions on the exam.
  He has to wear a uniform in school.

- We often use **have to** when we talk about laws or rules.
  You have to get good exam results to get into this college.
  He's angry because he has to take his hat off in school.

- **Have to** is follow by an infinitive without *to*.

- We use **don't have to** to say that it is not necessary to do something but that you can do it if you want.
  You don't have to help me with my experiment.
  She doesn't have to get up early tomorrow.

- Question words go at the beginning of the question.
  How much homework do you have to do every day?
  When do we have to make a decision?

- We use **can't** and **must not** to say something is prohibited by law or rules.
  I can't take my phone to school – it's the rule.
  You must not use your calculator during the exam.

- We use **need to** to express necessity in the present. We use **don't need to** to show a lack of necessity.
  I need to get home before my parents get angry.
  They don't need to leave now. It's still early.

- We use **should**(**'nt**) and **ought to** to give advice. **Should**(**'nt**) and **ought to** both mean "I (don't) think it's a good idea for someone to do this."
  You should take the bus. It will be faster.
  They shouldn't eat that. They're going to get sick.
  We ought to pay attention. This might be on the exam.

Past Obligation

- We use **had to** to say that it was necessary to do something in the past.
  I had to leave school early because I wasn't feeling well.
  They didn't have to come, but they did.
  Did you have to do chores when you were younger?
  Before we took the exam, we had to study a lot.

GRAMMAR PRACTICE

Modals of Deduction and Possibility

1 (Circle) the correct options.

1 I'm not sure, but I think this gold (may not)/ can't be real.

2 Reading in bed at night *can* / *must* help you fall asleep faster.

3 I don't know what's in the box. It *could* / *can* be a present.

4 Harry failed two exams. He *couldn't* / *can't* be very happy.

5 Take a drink of water. You *might* / *must* be very thirsty after the game.

6 The doctor's not very sure. She says it *might* / *must* be serious.

2 Use the prompts to write the second sentence.

1 I haven't eaten all day. You / be very hungry

   You must be very hungry.

2 It's eleven o'clock at night. Freya / be in bed

   _____

3 I feel sick. You / need to sit down

   _____

4 That boy looks like Freddie, but Freddie's in Mexico. That / be Freddie

   _____

5 Max got up late. He / not arrive on time for his first class

   _____

6 That cheese is three weeks old! It / be very smelly

   _____

Obligation, Prohibition, Necessity, and Advice

3 Are the sentences about obligation (*O*), prohibition (*P*), necessity (*N*), or advice (*A*)?

1 You must not use your phone in class.   P

2 I probably don't need to wear a coat today.   ___

3 I think Lauren should study engineering.   ___

4 You ought to try turning the computer off.   ___

5 You must write at least 100 words.   ___

6 What do I have to do to be successful?   ___

4 Complete the email with the phrases in the box.

> don't have to worry   ~~don't need to bring~~
> have to take   must not forget
> need to pack   ought to buy

Hi Evelyn,

I'm so glad you're coming to visit us. It's really warm here, so you ¹ _don't need to bring_ a coat. However, you ² _____ your swimsuit because we're going to the beach. We'll ³ _____ the train, so I ⁴ _____ our tickets tomorrow. You ⁵ _____ about bringing a towel because we have a lot, but you ⁶ _____ your sunscreen!

See you on Friday!

5 Complete the second sentence so that it means the same as the first. Use no more than three words.

1 Don't shout. I can hear everything you're saying.

   You ___ _don't need_ ___ to shout because I can hear everything you say.

2 It's not a very good idea to call him now.

   You probably _____ him now.

3 I had an appointment with the doctor yesterday.

   I _____ and see the doctor yesterday.

4 There's no need to worry about making lunch.

   You _____ to worry about making lunch.

5 No running in the hallways.

   Students _____ in the hallways.

6 That car must be very expensive.

   That car _____ cheap.

Past Obligation

6 Complete the sentences about past obligations with the correct form of *have to* and the verb in parentheses.

1 Julieta _____ (go) to school early on Thursday.

2 Did students _____ (gather) in the auditorium?

3 She _____ (not write) another paper.

The Passive

Simple Present		
Spanish	is	spoken in many countries.
Tigers	aren't	found in Africa.

Simple Past		
Writing	was	invented in Asia.
Planes	weren't	used until the 1900s.

Will		
The prize	will be	awarded next week.
The food	won't be	served until 10 p.m.

Questions			
Will	your project	be	finished by next week?

- We use the **passive** when we don't know or are not interested in who or what does an action.
- To form the **passive**, we use the appropriate form of **to be** + **past participle**.
  Millions of emails are written every day.
  Brian wasn't invited to the party.
  The microwave will be repaired tomorrow.
- We use the **simple present passive** to talk about facts in the present.
  English is spoken in most hotels and tourist offices.
- We use the **simple past passive** to talk about facts in the past.
  The first video game console was made in 1972.
- We use **will** with the **passive** to talk about facts and actions we believe will happen in the future.
  Results will be emailed to students next week.
- We use **by** with the **passive** to show who or what was responsible for an action.
  The book was written by a marketing expert.
- To form questions in the present and past, we use the appropriate form of **to be** + **subject** + **past participle**. We put *Wh-* question words before **be**.
  Was the light bulb really invented by Edison?
  Where is the most coffee drunk in the world?
- To form questions with **will**, we use **will** + **subject** + **be** + **past participle**.
  When will the next drama club meeting be held?

Question Tags

Main Clause	*To Be* / *To Do* / *To Have* / Modal + Subject Pronoun
They aren't ready,	are they?
They are ready,	aren't they?
We don't need a pencil,	do we?
We need a pen,	don't we?
He was sick,	wasn't he?
He wasn't sick,	was he?
She can't run a marathon,	can she?
She can run a marathon,	can't she?
You won't be late,	will you?
You'll be late,	won't you?
You haven't seen it,	have you?
You've seen it,	haven't you?

- We use **question tags** at the end of statements to invite a response from the listener.
  A You're an athlete, aren't you?
  B Yes, I am.
- To create **question tags**, we use **to be**, **to do**, **to have**, or a **modal verb**, plus a **subject**. The subject is normally a pronoun.
- Positive sentences have negative question tags and negative sentences have positive tags.
- When we use the auxiliary verbs **to be**, **to do**, **to have**, a **modal verb**, or the main verb **to be** in the main clause, this verb is used in the tag.

GRAMMAR PRACTICE

The Passive

1 Complete the sentences with the passive form of the verbs in parentheses.

1 Our groceries ___will be delivered___ (deliver) to our house tomorrow morning.

2 These problems _____ (solve) a long time ago.

3 _____ phone batteries _____ (produce) in this factory?

4 A lot of time _____ (waste) if we don't do something now.

5 It was delicious. The meat _____ (chop) into small pieces.

6 My computer _____ (not connect) to Wi-Fi.

2 Use the prompts to write questions in the passive. Use the tense in parentheses.

1 When / the books / deliver / ? (past)
   When were the books delivered?

2 Why / flies / attract / to the smell of food / ? (present)
   _____

3 How / these images / create / ? (past)
   _____

4 Where / we / pick up / after the museum visit / ? (will)
   _____

5 How / the meat / cook / ? (past)
   _____

6 When / a time machine / develop / ? (will)
   _____

3 Rewrite the sentences in the passive.

1 This lake supplies water to our town.
   Water _is supplied to our town from this lake._

2 They will send your grades to you in a week.
   Your grades _____

3 We measured the ingredients very carefully.
   The ingredients _____

4 They grill the fish over a fire.
   The fish _____

4 Complete the text with the passive form of the verbs in parentheses.

The city of Dubai is incredible. Before oil [1] _was discovered_ (discover) in 1966, it was a small town, but it [2] _____ (develop) into a modern city where millions of tourists [3] _____ (attract) to its shopping malls. In 1999, the seven-star Burj Al Arab [4] _____ (complete), and the 828-meter tall Burj Khalifa [5] _____ (open) in 2010. A new city with air conditioning [6] _____ (plan) for the future. Hotels and apartments [7] _____ (connect) with seven kilometers of stores.

Question Tags

5 Complete the questions with the correct verbs.

1 James ___isn't___ coming to lunch tomorrow, is he?

2 They _____ have to take the train, do they?

3 You _____ deliver the message later, won't you?

4 Robbie _____ going to call us today, wasn't he?

5 They _____ flying to Spain, are they?

6 She _____ be able to play, will she?

7 You _____ yoga every day, don't you?

8 Felicia _____ in class yesterday, was she?

6 Complete the questions with the correct questions tags.

1 You don't know the answer, ___do you___ ?

2 Dad picked up his car from the garage, _____ ?

3 Everyone knows the answer, _____ ?

4 They can't see the screen, _____ ?

5 Elena doesn't want to help us, _____ ?

6 You won't tell anyone what I told you, _____ ?

7 Grace listens to classical music a lot, _____ ?

8 You can't be in two places at once, _____ ?

First Conditional

- We use **first conditional** sentences to talk about possible situations in the present or future and say what we think the result will be.
- We often use **if** + **simple present** to describe the possible action or event.
  We'll find tickets if we go online at 7 a.m.
- We can use **unless** + **simple present** instead of **if not**.
  Unless we hurry up, we'll miss the bus.
- We use **will/won't** + **infinitive** when we are sure of the result and **may** or **might** + **infinitive** when we are less sure.
  If we don't leave now, we won't catch the 8:30 train.
  If my uncle doesn't feel better, he may not travel.
- When we use **if** to start the sentence, we use a comma between the two parts.
  If I have enough money, I'll go to the concert.
- We normally use **will** to make first conditional questions. It is unusual to use **may** or **might**.
  Will you practice with me this evening if you have time?

Second Conditional

- We use **second conditional** sentences to talk about imaginary situations and the possible consequences.
- We use **if** + **simple past** to describe the imaginary situation and **would**, **could**, or **might** for the consequence.
  If I didn't have a cat, I'd get a rabbit.
- We use **would** (**not**) when we are sure of the consequence.
  He would do better in school if he didn't spend all his time playing basketball.
- We use **could** (**not**) to express a possibility or ability as a consequence.
  If it was Friday night, we could go to the movies.
- We use **might** (**not**) to show we are less sure about the consequence.
  If I had more free time, I might take up the guitar.
- We can use **was** or **were** in the **if-** part of the sentence with *I*, *he/she*, and *it*.
  If it wasn't/weren't so spicy, I could finish it.
  I wouldn't say anything if I were/was you.

Third Conditional

Possible Situation in the Past	Imaginary Consequence
(*if* + past perfect)	(*would have* + infinitive)
If I had seen your message,	I would have called you.
If I hadn't seen your message,	I wouldn't have called you.
Imaginary Consequence	**Possible Situation in the Past**
(*would have* + infinitive)	(*if* + past perfect)
I would have called you	if I had seen your message.
I wouldn't have called you	if I hadn't seen your message.
Questions	
If he had been the chef,	what would he have prepared?
If you had let me help you,	wouldn't you have done better?

- We use the **third conditional** to talk about possible or imaginary situations in the past and the imaginary past consequences.
  If you hadn't read the story, the ending of the movie would have been a surprise.
  They would have found the exam easy if they'd worked harder.
- We use **if** + **past perfect** to describe a possible or imaginary past situation.
  If I hadn't missed the shot, we would have won the game.
  The book would have been better if the hero hadn't guessed that Jason was the bad guy.
- We use **would** (**not**) + **have** + **past participle** when we are sure of the imaginary past consequence.
  We would have seen his new car if he'd been at home.
  If she'd won the game, she wouldn't have been sad.
- We often use the **third conditional** to talk about things we regret doing.
  If I hadn't posted that photo, my parents wouldn't have found out.
  My sunglasses wouldn't have broken if I hadn't left them on the sofa.

GRAMMAR PRACTICE

First Conditional

1 Match the beginnings of the sentences with the ends.

1 If I get lost on the way,
2 If you season the chicken first,
3 Sean won't come to lunch
4 We might solve the problem faster
5 Unless you listen to the teacher,
6 They'll go sailing

a you won't understand.
b unless we go for pizza.
c it might taste better.
d unless it rains.
e I'll call you.
f if we sit down and talk.

2 Complete the sentences with the correct form of the verbs in parentheses.

1 If you _____listen_____ (listen) very carefully, you ____'ll hear____ (hear) a bird singing.
2 You _____ (not understand) Molly unless you _____ (get) to know her better.
3 Ruby _____ (not have) fun unless she _____ (join) in the game.
4 If Jason _____ (waste) any more time, he _____ (be) late for school.
5 We _____ (not be) able to watch the video unless we _____ (connect) to Wi-Fi.

Second Conditional

3 Circle the correct options.

1 If you *had* / *have* a new dog, what *you would* / *would you* name it?
2 If Brian *would go* / *went* to bed earlier, he *wasn't* / *wouldn't* always be late for school.
3 If I *could* / *can* have any job, I *'d work* / *worked* in a chocolate factory.
4 What *would you* / *did you* do if you *would find* / *found* a phone on the street?
5 If my mom *doesn't* / *didn't* work so hard, I think she *'d* / *'ll* be a lot happier.

4 Use the prompts to write second conditional questions.

1 If there / be / no electricity for a week, what / you / do / ?
If there was no electricity for a week, what would you do?
2 If animals / can communicate / with humans, what / they / say / ?
_____
3 you / go / to Mars / if / you / have / the chance / ?
_____
4 What / you / do / all day if you / live / on a desert island / ?
_____

Third Conditional

5 Complete the sentences with the correct form of the verbs in parentheses.

1 If you ____had taken____ (take) more interest in the subject, you ___wouldn't have failed___ (not fail) the exam.
2 I _____ (not get) lost if you _____ (not tell) me to turn left.
3 Henry _____ (finish) the marathon if we _____ (encourage) him a bit more.
4 We _____ (not miss) our stop if we _____ (not fall) asleep on the bus.
5 What _____ (happen) if Rocio _____ (press) that button?

6 Complete the third conditional sentences in the conversation with the correct form of the verbs in the box.

buy   give   go   ~~invite~~   look   not have   not hurt

SARA If Alice [1] ____had invited____ you to her party, [2] _____ you _____ ?

DANY Of course. And I [3] _____ her a nice present for her birthday.

SARA Really? What [4] _____ you _____ for her?

DANY I probably [5] _____ for something small, like some earrings.

SARA So, why didn't she invite you?

DANY It's a long story. But if I [6] _____ her feelings when she needed me to be her friend, we [7] _____ that big argument a few weeks ago.

GRAMMAR REFERENCE

Gerunds and Infinitives

Gerunds

- We can use a **gerund** as a noun and to make noun phrases.
  Running is great exercise.
  My favorite free-time activity is kitesurfing.
  Being the youngest child can be difficult sometimes.
  They think having a school dance is a terrible idea.

- We also use **gerunds** after prepositions.
  My aunt isn't very good at cooking, but she tries very hard.
  They spend a lot of money on buying clothes.
  We're thinking of giving up singing lessons.
  I'm looking forward to seeing you this summer.

- We use **gerunds** after certain verbs and expressions. Some common verbs and expressions that are followed by a gerund are *avoid, finish, enjoy, practice, miss, be good/bad at, can't stand,* and *don't mind.*
  They enjoy working on the same team.
  I don't mind helping you clean your room.

- With most verbs, we add **-ing** to the **infinitive** (without *to*).
  eat – eating   watch – watching   buy – buying

- For verbs ending in **-e**, we remove the **-e** and add **-ing**.
  have – having   write – writing   save – saving

- For verbs ending in a **vowel** and a **consonant**, we usually double the consonant and add **-ing**.
  get – getting   run – running   shop – shopping

- In American English, when words end in a **vowel** + **l**, the **l** is not doubled.
  travel – traveling   cancel – canceling

Infinitives

- We usually use the **infinitive with to** after adjectives.
  He was lucky to get tickets for the show.
  I'm very pleased to meet you!
  My teacher's very easy to talk to.

- We also use the **infinitive with to** after certain verbs. Some common verbs that are followed by an **infinitive with to** are *decide, want, refuse, hope, would like.*
  Kaitlyn decided to help me with my homework.
  We would like to buy two tickets, please.
  They refused to come with us.

- Some verbs need an object before the **infinitive with to**.
  My mom taught me to ride a bike.
  I didn't invite Elizabeth to come with us.

- Some verbs can have an object before **the infinitive with to**.
  They asked us to turn the music down.
  She'd like everyone to arrive by 8 a.m.

- We can use a **gerund** or **infinitive** after *remember, forget,* and *stop,* but it changes the meaning.
  Remember to do your assignment. (= Don't forget to do it.)
  Do you remember feeling so happy after we won? (= Do you have a memory of that moment?)
  Don't forget your book bag. (= Bring your book bag.)
  We'll never forget winning the championship. (= We'll always have a memory of that moment.)
  We stopped to eat something on our trip. (= We paused for a moment.)
  They stopped eating junk food last year. (= They quit eating junk food.)

Subject and Object Questions

- When we use **subject questions**, we are trying to find out information about the subject of the question. We don't use an auxiliary verb (*do, does, did*), the word order is inverted, and the *Wh-* word becomes the subject of the sentence.
  Who ate the last piece of cake?
  What happened?

- When we use **object questions**, we are trying to find out information about the object of the question and we use an auxiliary verb (*do, does, did*).
  Who does Tania like? (= We want to know who Tania likes.)
  What did Brad want? (= We want to know what Brad wanted.)

- To compare **subject and object questions** that are similar:
  Topic: *Mike likes eating vegetables.*
  Who likes eating vegetables? (subject question)
  (*Who* = *Mike*)
  What does Mike like eating? (object question)
  (*What* = *likes eating vegetables*)

GRAMMAR PRACTICE

Gerunds and Infinitives

1 Complete the sentences with the gerund or infinitive form of the verbs in parentheses.

1 It's easy ___to get___ (get) lost in this city.
2 Kyle refuses _____ (help) me with the project.
3 _____ (be) a police officer can be a dangerous job.
4 My mom has decided _____ (sell) her car.
5 My grandmother enjoys _____ (listen) to the radio.
6 Are you afraid of _____ (fly)?

2 Complete the sentences with the gerund or infinitive form of the verbs in the box.

> drive   go   play   ~~show~~   solve   take   use

1 I'll be happy ___to show___ you around my school.
2 We're looking forward to _____ skiing this winter.
3 Have you finished _____ my computer?
4 Would you like _____ video games later?
5 _____ public transportation in big cities is often quicker than _____ .
6 This problem might be complicated _____ .

3 Complete the email with the correct form of the verbs in parentheses.

Hi Hollie,

I hope you're well. Do you remember [1] ___inviting___ (invite) me [2] _____ (come) and stay with you a few months ago? Well, I'm really pleased [3] _____ (tell) you that I'm going to be in the U.S. next month. My parents have decided [4] _____ (send) me to Boston for a month because they would like me [5] _____ (practice) my English. I don't mind [6] _____ (travel) to Boston at all. In fact, I'm really looking forward to [7] _____ (see) you again.

I really hope [8] _____ (hear) from you soon.

Love, Amber

4 (Circle) the correct options.

1 I don't remember *to tell* / (*telling*) you what Sarah told me.
2 Have you forgotten *to do* / *doing* your homework again?
3 Samuel can't stop *to listen* / *listening* to that song. He loves it.
4 We worked on the project all day, and we only stopped *to eat* / *eating* lunch.
5 I've never forgotten *to win* / *winning* that art contest.
6 Sophie didn't remember *to set* / *setting* her alarm clock, so she was late.

Subject and Object Questions

5 Write subject questions for these answers.

1 <u>William</u> decided not to go to the party.
   Who decided not to go to the party?
2 Class <u>5A</u> is going to the National Museum tomorrow.
   _____
3 <u>Nobody</u> sent me a message on my birthday.
   _____
4 <u>A rock</u> fell on my dad's car.
   _____

6 (Circle) the correct options.

1 Who (*invented*) / *did invent* the telephone?
2 What *studies your sister* / *does your sister study*?
3 Who *is going* / *he going* to tell George?
4 What *did happen* / *happened* when she found out?
5 Who *can ask* / *can we ask* to come and help us tomorrow?
6 Which team *beat* / *did you beat* last year?

Defining Relative Clauses

- We use **defining relative clauses** to give essential information about a person, place, or thing.
  My aunt has a friend who makes great cookies.
  This is the movie that I told you about.

- We use **relative pronouns** at the beginning of relative clauses. We do <u>not</u> repeat the subject pronoun when the subject of the pronoun and following clause are the same.
  I know a lot of people who live in Veracruz.
  (NOT I know a lot of people who they live in Veracruz.)

- We use **who** or **that** to talk about people.
  The woman who/that lives next door is very friendly.
  I like the new person who/that works in the café.

- We use **that** to talk about things.
  I don't enjoy books that have sad endings.
  He wants to buy some boots that he can wear with his new hat.

- We use **where** to talk about places.
  That's the office where my uncle works.
  Let's go to the restaurant where I had my birthday dinner.

- We use **whose** to talk about possessions.
  Do you remember the boy whose phone was lost?

Non-Defining Relative Clauses

- We use **non-defining relative clauses** to give extra information about a person or thing. We don't need it to understand who or what is being referred to. It is not necessary information. Non-defining relative clauses are introduced by a relative pronoun, and we use commas around them.
  Ms. Parker, who studied in Italy, is my teacher.
  They just visited Madrid, where Javier is from.
  Last night, we had dinner at John's Pizza Parlor, which we'd never tried before.
  My dad, whose name is Wayne, is 45 years old.

- We don't use **that** to introduce a non-defining relative clause. We use **which**, not *that*, for things.
  Sam, who scored three goals in the first game, was amazing.
  (NOT Sam, that scored three goals in the first game, was amazing.)
  We're having lasagna, which is my favorite dish, for dinner.
  (NOT We're having lasagna, that is my favorite dish, for dinner.)

Indefinite Pronouns

anybody	everybody	nobody	somebody
anyone	everyone	no one	someone
anything	everything	nothing	something
anywhere	everywhere	nowhere	somewhere

- We use **indefinite pronouns** to refer to people, places, and things in a general way. To create **indefinite pronouns**, we combine *any*, *every*, *no*, and *some* with *body*, *one*, *thing*, or *where*. We write them as one single word, except for *no one*.
  Is anybody here? = Is anyone here?
  Everybody is late today. = Everyone is late today.
  Nobody was there last night. = No one was there last night.
  Can somebody help me? = Can someone help me?
  Is something wrong? = Is anything wrong?

Reflexive Pronouns

I	→	myself	it	→	itself
you	→	yourself	we	→	ourselves
he	→	himself	you	→	yourselves
she	→	herself	they	→	themselves

- We use **reflexive pronouns** when the subject and the object of a verb are the same.
  I sing to myself when I'm alone.
  (NOT I sing to me when I'm alone.)
  She bought herself a new shirt.
  (NOT She bought she a new shirt.)

- We can also use **reflexive pronouns** to emphasize that someone did something alone, without help.
  He didn't buy the cookies – he made them himself. He's good at baking.

Reciprocal Pronouns

- We use **each other** or **one another** when each of the two (or more) subjects do the verb to the other subject(s).
  Dave and Ellen sent each other presents. (Dave sent Ellen a present, and Ellen sent Dave a present.)
  The triplets really love each other. They're always together.
  We message one another all the time.

GRAMMAR PRACTICE

Defining Relative Clauses

1 Match the beginnings of the sentences with the ends.

1 Is that the movie that
2 Rugby is a sport that
3 This is the park that
4 We have a neighbor who
5 This company has a slogan that
6 That's the student whose

a has a big lake in the middle of it.
b stars Daniel Radcliffe?
c says, "Power to shoes."
d plays the drums.
e chair broke in French class.
f is played between teams of 15 players.

2 Complete the sentences with the correct relative pronoun.

1 I really like that new ad _____that_____ has a song by Mark Ronson.
2 That's the movie theater _____ Mark dropped a whole bucket of popcorn.
3 She's the teacher _____ laptop was stolen from the classroom.
4 It's a radio station _____ plays mostly rock and pop.
5 This is the hotel _____ we stayed on our last vacation.

Non-Defining Relative Clauses

3 Correct the mistake in each sentence.

1 That ad, ~~what~~ was on TV last night, was really funny. _____which_____
2 This fish, which we bought it in the supermarket, was very expensive. _____
3 Maya, who's dad comes from Australia, works in marketing. _____
4 Theo's review of the movie, that Lucas sent me, was hilarious. _____
5 Dublin, which Mike has lived since he was five, is the capital of Ireland. _____
6 My friend, which I was following on social media, has blocked me. _____

Indefinite Pronouns

4 Complete the sentences with the correct indefinite pronoun.

1 I don't know _____anything_____ about advertising.
2 My sister deleted _____ on my computer by accident.
3 There are ads for that brand _____!
4 _____ at the party was really nice. I had a great time.
5 The teacher wanted _____ to answer the question, but _____ knew the answer.
6 Paula says she can't find her glasses _____.

Reflexive and Reciprocal Pronouns

5 Complete the conversation with the pronouns in the box.

> anything   anywhere   each other   ~~everyone~~
> himself   nobody   someone   themselves

MIA   So how was Phil's party?
NOAH   Oh, it was a lot of fun. [1] _____Everyone_____ really enjoyed [2] _____. And the food was delicious.
MIA   Phil's a good cook. Did he make it all [3] _____?
NOAH   Yes, … well he says [4] _____ helped him, but I think his sister made the cake.
MIA   So, did [5] _____ interesting happen?
NOAH   Not really … Sam and Katie had had an argument and weren't speaking to [6] _____. Oh, and Carmen lost her coat, and she couldn't find it [7] _____. It turned out that [8] _____ had taken it home by mistake!

Reported Speech: Verb Patterns
Independent Clauses

Direct Speech	Reported Speech
Simple Present "I **want** some new shoes."	**Simple Past** He said (that) he **wanted** some new shoes.
Simple Past "I **had** a great time."	**Past Perfect** She said (that) she **had had** a great time.
Present Perfect "We'**ve** just **seen** a show about a fire."	**Past Perfect** She said (that) they **had** just **seen** a show about a fire.
Present Continuous "We'**re growing** our own vegetables."	**Past Continuous** He said (that) they **were growing** their own vegetables.
will "They **will** need to bring a laptop."	*would* She said (that) they **would** need to bring a laptop.
can "You **can** do it."	*could* He said (that) I **could** do it.
must "We **must** buy some bread."	*had to* She said (that) we **had to** buy some bread.
have to "I **have to** wear a uniform."	*had to* She said (that) she **had to** wear a uniform.

- We can report speech using an **independent clause** and **that**. *That* is optional.
- When we report somebody's words, we often have to change the verb forms – see the table above for how the verb forms change.
- We often need to change pronouns in reported speech.
  *"**You** have to leave before 11 p.m." – He said (that) **we** had to leave before 11 p.m.*

Gerunds and Infinitives

- We can also report statements using gerunds (**subject + past tense verb** + **gerund**), prepositions with gerunds (**subject + past tense verb** + **preposition + gerund**), or infinitives (**subject + past tense verb + infinitive**).

- **... + gerund**

  *"Let's take the bus instead of walking." – She **suggested taking** the bus instead of walking.*

- **... + preposition + gerund**

  *Joe said, "I insist we cut the lawn." – Joe **insisted on cutting** the lawn.*

- **... + infinitive**

  *"I can carry the bag for you." – She **offered to carry** the bag for me.*

Reported Questions

- When we report questions, we usually make the same changes to the verb forms, pronouns, and time references as when we report statements.

- When we report questions with a *Wh-* word, we don't add an auxiliary verb and the word order is the same as in affirmative sentences.
  He asked me what I'd done over the weekend.
  (NOT ~~He asked me what had I done over the weekend.~~)
  Connor asked when the school trip was.
  (NOT ~~Connor asked when was the school trip.~~)

- When we report *Yes/No* questions, we use **if**.
  "Did you tell the truth?" – They asked him if he'd told the truth.

- We don't use a question mark when we report questions.
  "Where did you go after school?" – My parents asked me where I'd been after school.

Indirect Questions

- **Indirect questions** are a type of reported question. We use indirect questions when we want to sound more polite or formal.
  How did you finish your homework so fast? – Would you mind telling me how you finished your homework so fast?

- When we ask indirect *Yes/No* questions, we use **if** or **whether**.
  Did they see the movie? – Do you know whether they saw the movie?

- We do not use the auxiliary verb *to do* in indirect questions.
  When does this class start? – Could you tell me when this class starts?
  (NOT ~~Could you tell me when does this class start?~~)

GRAMMAR PRACTICE

Reported Speech: Verb Patterns

1 Write the statements in reported speech.

1 "I don't want to go out for lunch."

   Alison said (that) she didn't want to go out for lunch.

2 "We won't waste any more time."

   They told us _____

3 "I can help you make lunch."

   Joshua said _____

4 "I haven't bought your birthday present yet."

   Andy said to Amy _____

5 "Heidi's moving to Australia next week."

   You told me _____

2 Complete the reported statements with two or three words.

1 "Write an essay about technology."

   The teacher told ___ _me to write_ ___ an essay about technology.

2 "Don't touch my new car!"

   My dad told _____ touch his new car!

3 "Tell them to keep the noise down."

   Martha told me _____ to keep the noise down.

4 "Don't say anything to Charlie about the concert."

   She _____ to say anything to Charlie about the concert.

3 Complete the reported statements with the correct form of the verbs in the box.

> ~~correct~~   drive   help   not tell   turn

1 Helen asked us _to correct_ her essay before she gave it to the teacher.

2 My friend's dad offered _____ us to school.

3 They suggested _____ Thomas what had happened.

4 When did Ethan offer _____ you with your math homework?

5 Who suggested _____ the computer on and off?

Reported Questions

4 Rewrite the questions in reported speech.

1 "Are you going to make dinner?" Jake asked Jazmin.

   Jake asked Jazmin if she was going to make dinner.

2 "What will make you change your mind?" Maria asked me.

   _____

3 "Have you ever been to Vienna?" I asked my friend.

   _____

4 "When is the next exam?" Leah asked the teacher.

   _____

5 "Do you change your mind often?" Josue asked her.

   _____

5 Correct the mistake in each sentence.

1 They asked us ~~could we~~ help them.   _if we could_

2 The teacher asked me why hadn't I done my homework. _____

3 The doctor asked me where it does hurt.

   _____

4 Paula wanted to know if could she borrow my phone. _____

5 My dad asked me what did happen.

   _____

Indirect Questions

6 Complete the second question so that it means the same as the first. Use no more than three words.

1 Can I try a piece of cake?

   Would you mind ___ _if I tried_ ___ a piece of cake?

2 When is the next bus?

   Could you _____ the next bus is?

3 Do you go out all the time?

   Can you tell me _____ out all the time?

4 Where's my hat?

   Do you _____ my hat is?

5 Is there a soccer game tonight?

   Would you mind telling me _____ a soccer game tonight?

LANGUAGE BANK

STARTER

Vocabulary
Travel

> accommodation   backpacking   resort
> sightseeing   tourist attractions   trip

Music and Theater

> audience   lines   part
> rehearsal   scene   show

Ways of Communicating

> describe   greet   post   shake hands
> shout   smile   translate   wave   whisper

Grammar in Action
Past and Present, Simple and Continuous
Present Perfect and Simple Past

Writing
Useful Language
Starting and Ending an Informal Email
Hello … / Hi …
How are you? / Thanks for your email. / How are things?
I'm writing to … / I just wanted to say …
See you soon. / Bye for now. / Write back soon.
Take care, … / Love, …

UNIT 1

Vocabulary
Describing Clothes and Shoes

> baggy   checkered   cotton   denim
> flowery   high-heeled   leather   long-sleeved
> plain   polka-dot   striped   tight

Verbs Related to Clothes and Shoes

> fit   fold   go out of style
> go with   hang up   look good on   match
> unzip   wear out   zip up

Grammar in Action
Present Perfect Simple and Present Perfect Continuous
Modifiers

Speaking
Everyday English
check out
fashion victim
in
out there

Useful Language
I don't know if …
I'm not a huge fan of …
I think maybe …
That's … uh … different!
They're not exactly my style.

Writing
Useful Language
Great post!
I had no idea that …
It got me thinking about …
Since reading your post, I've …
Thanks for sharing!
We decided to …

LANGUAGE BANK

UNIT 2

Vocabulary
Phrasal Verbs: Changes

> do without   end up   go back   go through
> look forward to   move out   move to
> settle down   sign up   try out
> turn down   turn out

Parts of Objects

> button   cord   cover   display   handle
> key   lens   lid   plug   strap

Grammar in Action
Used To, *Would*, and Simple Past
Past Perfect with *Never*, *Ever*, *Already*, *By* (*Then*),
By the Time

Speaking
Everyday English
all over again
I'm not surprised.
old-school
That's it.

Useful Language
Is it some kind of …?
I've messed it up.
Like this, you mean?
What you do is, you …
You'll have to …

Writing
Useful Language
first
in addition
in conclusion
second
therefore
this means that

UNIT 3

Vocabulary
Cooking Verbs

> bake   boil   chop   fry   grate
> grill   overcook   peel   roast
> season   slice   spread

Quantities

> a bag of   a chunk of   a cup of   a handful of
> a piece of   a pinch of   a slice of
> a splash of   a spoonful of   a sprinkle of

Grammar in Action
Future Forms
Future Continuous and Future Perfect

Speaking
Everyday English
a piece of cake
forever
Is that it?
tasty

Useful Language
Don't forget to … (+ verb)
Once that's done, …
Start by … (+ -*ing*)
While that's … (+ -*ing*)
You'll need …

Writing
Useful Language
… is here to stay
… isn't going anywhere
Watch this space
… will be around forever
… will be the norm

LANGUAGE BANK

UNIT 4

Vocabulary
The Five Senses

> feel   feel like   look   look like
> smell   smell like   sound
> sound like   taste   taste like   touch

Describing Texture, Sound, Taste, Etc.

> colorful   faint   rough   sharp   shiny
> smelly   smooth   sour   spicy   transparent

Grammar in Action
Modals of Deduction and Possibility
Obligation, Prohibition, Necessity, and Advice
Past Obligation

Speaking

Everyday English
Bingo!
I give up!
I guess so.
nice and warm/hot, etc.
Sure, why not?

Useful Language
Guess again.
Guess what it is / they are.
I guess they must be …
Perhaps it's something (+ *adjective*)
They're definitely some kind of …

Writing
Useful Language
According to …
and grew up in …
At the age of …
including …
… is known as …
… was born on …

UNIT 5

Vocabulary
Processes

> attract   collect   communicate   connect
> create   deliver   develop   measure
> produce   solve   supply   waste

Extreme Adjectives

> awful   boiling   deafening   enormous
> fascinating   freezing   gorgeous
> marvelous   stunning   terrifying

Grammar in Action
The Passive
Question Tags

Speaking

Everyday English
… and everything
I'd say it was …
Oh, man
Um, not exactly.
Wanna …?

Useful Language
Are you kidding me?
I can't believe you actually …
I find that hard to believe.
Seriously?
You can't be serious.

Writing
Useful Language
… deserves to win because …
I'm absolutely certain that …
The highlight of a visit to … is …
the … that impressed me the most was …
Without a doubt, …

LANGUAGE BANK

UNIT 6

Vocabulary
Verb Collocations with *To Get*, *To Take*, and *To Have*

get a lot out of   get bored   get lost
get on my nerves   get to know
have doubts   have fun   have the chance
take advantage of   take an interest in
take pleasure in   take risks

Inspiration and Challenge

Nouns	Verbs
bravery	achieve
challenge	encourage
determination	inspire
obstacle	overcome
opportunity	support

Grammar in action
First and Second Conditional
Third Conditional

Speaking
Everyday English
Come on!
Good for you!
not really
seriously
You've got to be kidding!

Useful Language
Encouraging
Don't worry, you'll be fine.
You can do it!
You'll feel really proud afterward.
You'll never know unless you try.
Responding
That's easy for you to say.
What if … ?

Writing
Useful Language
For example, … / For instance, … / such as …
Furthermore, … / On the one hand, …
I personally believe (that) …
On the other hand, …
In conclusion, …

UNIT 7

Vocabulary
Feelings

amused   annoyed   down   eager   glad
grateful   hopeful   hurt   insecure
peaceful   ridiculous   satisfied   thrilled

Expressions with *Heart* and *Mind*

bear in mind   be close to my heart
break someone's heart   change my mind
cross my mind   have something on my mind
learn by heart   make up my mind
put my heart into something   slip my mind

Grammar in Action
Gerunds and Infinitives
Subject and Object Questions

Speaking
Everyday English
kind of harsh
Don't mention it.
I swear
stressed out
That's kind of you …

Useful Language
I can imagine.
Is there anything I can do to help?
It'll be alright, you'll see.
That's not very nice.
What's the matter?

Writing
Useful Language
It might be better (not) to …
It would definitely help to …
I would recommend … (+ *-ing*)
Whatever you do, don't …
Why don't you suggest … (+ *-ing*)?

LANGUAGE BANK

UNIT 8

Vocabulary
Advertising

> ad   ad blocker   advertise   brand
> buyer   influence   logo   marketing company
> product   review   seller   slogan

Internet Verbs

> build up   comment on   delete   follow
> post   shut down   subscribe to
> switch off   switch on   vlog

Grammar in Action
Defining Relative Clauses
Non-Defining Relative Clauses
Indefinite, Reflexive, and Reciprocal Pronouns

Speaking
Everyday English
handy
I don't have a clue.
no-brainer
What's up?

Useful Language
I can't recommend it/them enough!
I don't know where to start!
Is it easy to use?
It's the best thing …
(It) would be ideal for …
You really ought to …

Writing
Useful Language
… is included.
It allows you to …
It is designed to be used …
One of its best features is …
The one thing that's missing is …

UNIT 9

Vocabulary
Reporting Verbs

> admit   announce   apologize   claim
> complain   confirm   deny   discover
> insist   promise   refuse   suggest

Adverbs of Time and Manner

> after a while   eventually   fluently
> gradually   nowadays   occasionally
> patiently   regularly   secretly   surprisingly

Grammar in Action
Reported Speech: Verb Patterns
Reported Questions
Indirect Questions

Speaking
Everyday English
Hey!
Let me guess.
show-off
kind of
to make matters worse

Useful Language
Basically, what happened was …
It was so (+ *adjective*)
So, anyway, …
The next thing I knew …
You'll never guess what happened …

Writing
Useful Language
A man/woman from …
He/She announced/explained/admitted that …
"…," he/she said
Surprisingly/Nowadays, etc., …
When asked … he/she answered/explained/said …

IRREGULAR VERBS

Infinitive	Simple Past	Past Participle
be	was/were	been
beat	beat	beaten
become	became	become
begin	began	begun
bite	bit	bitten
blow	blew	blown
break	broke	broken
bring	brought	brought
build	built	built
buy	bought	bought
catch	caught	caught
choose	chose	chosen
come	came	come
cost	cost	cost
cut	cut	cut
do	did	done
draw	drew	drawn
drink	drank	drunk
drive	drove	driven
eat	ate	eaten
fall	fell	fallen
feel	felt	felt
fight	fought	fought
find	found	found
fly	flew	flown
forget	forgot	forgotten
get	got	gotten
give	gave	given
go	went	gone
grow	grew	grown
hang	hung	hung
have	had	had
hear	heard	heard
hide	hid	hidden
hit	hit	hit
hold	held	held
hurt	hurt	hurt
keep	kept	kept
know	knew	known
leave	left	left
lend	lent	lent

Infinitive	Simple Past	Past Participle
let	let	let
lie	lied	lied
light	lit	lit
lose	lost	lost
make	made	made
mean	meant	meant
meet	met	met
pay	paid	paid
put	put	put
read	read	read
ride	rode	ridden
ring	rang	rung
rise	rose	risen
run	ran	run
say	said	said
see	saw	seen
sell	sold	sold
send	sent	sent
shine	shone	shone
shoot	shot	shot
show	showed	shown
shut	shut	shut
sing	sang	sung
sit	sat	sat
sleep	slept	slept
speak	spoke	spoken
spend	spent	spent
stand	stood	stood
steal	stole	stolen
swim	swam	swum
take	took	taken
teach	taught	taught
tear	tore	torn
tell	told	told
think	thought	thought
throw	threw	thrown
understand	understood	understood
wake	woke	woken
wear	wore	worn
win	won	won
write	wrote	written

ACKNOWLEDGMENTS

The authors and publishers acknowledge the following sources of copyright material and are grateful for the permissions granted. While every effort has been made, it has not always been possible to identify the sources of all the material used, or to trace all copyright holders. If any omissions are brought to our notice, we will be happy to include the appropriate acknowledgements on reprinting & in the next update to the digital edition, as applicable.

Key: **SU** = Starter Unit, **U** = Unit

Photography

The following photographs are sourced from Getty Images.

SU: Harald Nachtmann/Moment; Anestis Karagiannopoulos/EyeEm; Matteo Colombo/DigitalVision; oleksii arseniuk/iStock/Getty Images Plus; Anastasiia_M/iStock/Getty Images Plus; chokkicx/DigitalVision Vectors; primeimages/iStock/Getty Images Plus; Nikada/iStock/Getty Images Plus; JohnnyGreig/E+; platongkoh/iStock/Getty Images Plus; Hans Neleman/Stone; Hemera Technologies/PhotoObjects.net; SDI Productions/E+; John Cancalosi/Photolibrary; Hill Street Studios/DigitalVision; **U1:** ArnaPhoto/iStock/Getty Images Plus; Sadeugra/E+; ferrantraite/iStock/Getty Images Plus; JackF/iStock/Getty Images Plus; Chiyacat/iStock/Getty Images Plus; rolfbodmer/E+; Jitalia17/E+; skodonnell/E+; CSA Images/Vetta; **U2:** Julie Moquet/EyeEm; Ariel Skelley/DigitalVision; JRL/The Image Bank/Getty Images Plus; Don Mason; Getty Images/Aurora Creative; Image Source; Ljupco/iStock/Getty Images Plus; slobo/iStock/Getty Images Plus; hh5800/iStock/Getty Images Plus; homydesign/iStock/Getty Images Plus; Bet_Noire/iStock/Getty Images Plus; Valerie Loiseleux/iStock/Getty Images Plus; Whiteway/iStock/Getty Images Plus; Getty Images/Caiaimage; Debrocke/ClassicStock/Archive Photos; kertlis/E+; PM Images/DigitalVision; Wan Muhammad Faisalludin Wan Azeland/EyeEm; Peter Dazeley/The Image Bank; Richard Newstead/Moment; Oliver Cleve/Photographer's Choice; TommL/E+; Nicholas Eveleigh/Photodisc; ET-ARTWORKS/DigitalVision Vectors; NiseriN/iStock/Getty Images Plus; **U3:** Getty Images/Dorling Kindersley; Guillermo Murcia/Moment Open; Jody Louie took this picture/Moment; Joy Skipper/Photolibrary; Giles Clarke/Getty Images News; Gavin Hellier/robertharding/Getty Images Plus; Rosemary Calvert/The Image Bank Unreleased; alantobey/E+; Anne Ackermann/DigitalVision; George Mdivanian/EyeEm; erierika/iStock/Getty Images Plus; Getty Images/StockFood; Simon McGill/Moment; Chris Everard/The Image Bank/Getty Images Plus; anna1311/iStock/Getty Images Plus; Christian Vierig/Getty Images Entertainment; Evgeniyaphotography/iStock/Getty Images Plus; -slav-/iStock/Getty Images Plus; imaginima/iStock/Getty Images Plus; H. Armstrong Roberts/ClassicStock/Archive Photos; Highwaystarz-Photography/iStock/Getty Images Plus; **U4:** Elizaveta Pahomova/EyeEm; kiszon pascal/Moment; Guillaume CHANSON/Moment; Kristina Strasunske/Moment; Getty Images/Caiaimage; Johann van Heerden/Moment Open; Nenov/Moment Open; briddy_/iStock/Getty Images Plus; Ed Freeman/Stone; Sally Anscombe/DigitalVision; Henrik Sorensen/DigitalVision; Glynne Joseph Pritchard/Moment Mobile; Noam Galai/Getty Images Entertainment; Toni Anne Barson/FilmMagic; Fuse/Corbis; **U5:** Danita Delimont/Gallo Images; Kevin Winter/Getty Images Entertainment; RusticFOTO/iStock/Getty Images Plus; Eerik/iStock/Getty Images Plus; Simon McGill/Moment; Stefan032/E+; kolderal/Moment; Joachim; Hiltmann Stefano Bianchetti/Corbis Historical; Brian Bumby/Moment; Arthit Somsakul/Moment; Thomas H. Mitchell/500px; Richard Geoffrey/EyeEm; **U6:** FatCamera/E+; sturti/E+; Getty Images/Bill Stormont; Pam Francis/Photographer's Choice/Getty Images Plus; Mark Newman/The Image Bank; Yulia337/iStock/Getty Images Plus; LauriPatterson/E+; Svein Nordrum/Moment; Mike Harrington/Stone; **U7:** AJ_Watt/E+; Purple Collar Pet Photography/Moment; g-stockstudio/iStock/Getty Images Plus; Thomas Barwick/DigitalVision; izusek/E+; Luxy Images; Maica/iStock/Getty Images Plus; PeopleImages/E+; Klaus Mellenthin; PetrMalyshev/iStock/Getty Images Plus; Tanya St/iStock/Getty Images Plus; **U8:** Bartosz Hadyniak/E+; Skarin/iStock/Getty Images Plus; Oleh Svetiukha/iStock/Getty Images Plus; Getty Images/Hero Images; ComicSans/iStock/Getty Images Plus; oleksii arseniuk/iStock/Getty Images Plus; IfH85/iStock/Getty Images Plus; bestbrk/iStock/Getty Images Plus; Oleksandr Hruts/iStock/Getty Images Plus; Katrin Ray Shumakov/Moment; burakpekakcan/E+; Mendelex_photography/iStock/Getty Images Plus; Hulton Deutsch/Corbis Historical; **U9:** Jim Arbogast/Photodisc; Patrick Foto/Getty Images; sturti/E+; Alex Ramsel/500px Prime; Highwaystarz-Photography/iStock/Getty Images Plus; Nastasic/iStock/Getty Images Plus; agafapaperiapunta/iStock Editorial; LazingBee/E+.

Cover design and illustrations: Collaborate Agency

Illustrations

U1: Claire Rollet; **U3:** Joanna Kerr; **U4:** Howarth from The Big Red illustration; **U6:** Claire Rollet; Joanna Kerr; **U8:** Joanna Kerr; **U9:** Claire Rollet.

Audio produced by Eastern Sky

Typesetting: Aphik, S.A. de C.V.

American English Consultant: Mandie Drucker

Freelance Editors: Sue Costello, Jacqueline French, Bastian Harris, and Penny Nicholson